Mary

Becoming a Girl of Faithfulness

DANNAH GRESH

with Hildsy Marie

MOODY PUBLISHERS

CHICAGO

Unless otherwise indicated, all Scripture quotations are taken from the *Holy Bible*, New Living Translation, copyright © 1996, 2004, 2015 by Tyndale House Foundation. Used by permission of Tyndale House Publishers, Carol Stream, Illinois 60188. All rights reserved.

Scripture quotations marked (ESV) are from the ESV® Bible (The Holy Bible, English Standard Version®), copyright © 2001 by Crossway, a publishing ministry of Good News Publishers. Used by permission. All rights reserved. The ESV text may not be quoted in any publication made available to the public by a Creative Commons license. The ESV may not be translated into any other language.

Scripture quotations marked (NIV) are taken from the Holy Bible, New International Version®, NIV®. Copyright © 1973, 1978, 1984, 2011 by Biblica, Inc.™ Used by permission of Zondervan. All rights reserved worldwide. www.zondervan.com The "NIV" and "New International Version" are trademarks registered in the United States Patent and Trademark Office by Biblica, Inc.™

Edited by Ashleigh Slater
Interior and cover design: Julia Ryan
Cover and interior illustrations: Julia Ryan
Interior illustration of pink flowers copyright © 2023 by windesign/ Shutterstock (289092644). All rights reserved.
Interior illustration of magnifying glass copyright © 2023 by M.Stasy/ Shutterstock (115513243). All rights reserved.
Interior illustration of treasure chest copyright © 2023 by Pagina/ Shutterstock (106348796). All rights reserved.
Interior illustration of autumn leaves copyright © 2023 by Green Flame/ Shutterstock (1493892203). All rights reserved.
Interior illustration of jigsaw puzzle pieces copyright © 2023 by ugurv/ Shutterstock (230789305). All rights reserved.
Interior illustration of stuffed animals copyright © 2023 by Pixavril/ Shutterstock (756677980). All rights reserved.

Printed by Versa Press in East Peoria, IL – May 2023

Library of Congress Cataloging-in-Publication Data

Names: Gresh, Dannah, 1967- author.
Title: Mary : becoming a girl of faithfulness / Dannah Gresh with Hildsy
   Marie.
Description: Chicago : Moody Publishers, [2023] | Includes bibliographical
   references. | Audience: Ages 8-12 | Summary: "In Mary, a six-week Bible
   study, you'll enter Mary's story and learn how you can become a girl of
   faithfulness. God chooses ordinary girls who are willing to say, "Yes."
   Mary's life proves that when a True Girl responds with faith in the
   moment, it brings a beautiful, forever blessing"-- Provided by
   publisher.
Identifiers: LCCN 2023004537 (print) | LCCN 2023004538 (ebook) | ISBN
   9780802422422 | ISBN 9780802499387 (ebook)
Subjects: LCSH: Mary, Blessed Virgin, Saint--Juvenile literature. |
   Constancy--Juvenile literature. | BISAC: JUVENILE NONFICTION / Religious
   / Christian / Inspirational | JUVENILE NONFICTION / Girls & Women
Classification: LCC BT607 .G69 2023 (print) | LCC BT607 (ebook) | DDC
   232.91--dc23/eng/20230202
LC record available at https://lccn.loc.gov/2023004537
LC ebook record available at https://lccn.loc.gov/2023004538

Originally delivered by fleets of horse-drawn wagons, the affordable paperbacks from D. L. Moody's publishing house resourced the church and served everyday people. Now, after more than 125 years of publishing and ministry, Moody Publishers' mission remains the same—even if our delivery systems have changed a bit. For more information on other books (and resources) created from a biblical perspective, go to: www.moodypublishers.com or write to:

Moody Publishers
820 N. LaSalle Boulevard
Chicago, IL 60610

1 3 5 7 9 10 8 6 4 2

Printed in the United States of America

Table of Contents

My Notes on Mary

As you study the life of Mary, you can come back to this page to write down important thoughts and observations about her and the most important people in her life. Turn here anytime you learn something you don't want to forget or when I remind you.

_____   _____   _____

{ Her Husband }   { The Mother of Jesus }   { Our Savior }

My Map of Mary's Road Trips

Mary was kind of a frequent traveler! As we study, you're going to fill this map with footprints to track her road trips. I'll tell you to turn to this page to do some special assignments from time to time.

NAZARETH

MEDITERRANEAN SEA

JERUSALEM

BETHLEHEM

HEBRON
THE HILL COUNTRY
OF JUDEA

JUDEA

Faithfulness Lessons

We're going to study the life of Mary to learn six important lessons about **faithfulness**. Sometimes I will invite you to come back to this page and write down what you're learning!

Faithfulness Lesson #1

Faithfulness Lesson #2

Faithfulness Lesson #6

Faithful

▸ **Fill in the blanks!**

Faithful: able to be _____ or _____ on.

Faithfulness Lesson #3

Faithfulness Lesson #4

Faithfulness Lesson #5

INTRODUCTION

How to Study the Bible
(Zooming, Zeroing & Zipping Basics!)

If you've never done a True Girl Bible study,
this introduction is really important.
It will explain our style of studying the Bible.

If you have done a True Girl Bible study before,
you can skip this and go straight to chapter 1.[1]

I'm so pumped that you've decided to dig into this Bible study to learn about the life and faithfulness of Mary! If you're here, you mayyyy have heard of something called the Bible. After all, it *is* the bestselling book in all of history. But, have you ever stopped and wondered: *What's with all the hype?!* Why is this book so special? Well, my friend, those are very good questions, and I'm so glad you asked!

What is the Bible, Really?

The Bible contains the story of God's relationship with His creation. Although it's all bound up together into one book that you can hold, the Bible is actually a collection of a bunch of different books written by many ancient writers. These books contain stories, poems, songs, prayers, and more. Some of these people wrote about their experiences with God, and some wrote about how they saw God's story playing out in front of them. Every word of the Bible is *inspired by* God, which means that God was leading the authors and telling them exactly what to write! That means the Bible is God's Word, so it's the ultimate source of truth! (After all, who knows it better than God?)

All Scripture is inspired by God and is useful to teach us what is true and to make us realize what is wrong in our lives. It corrects us when we are wrong and teaches us to do what is right. (2 Timothy 3:16)

Fast-forward to today, and guess what? The authors who wrote down the Bible may not be around anymore, but the Bible certainly is. God's story isn't over yet and is continuing with you! It's true. So, as we participate in the story of God's relationship with His creation, we look to the Bible to find the truth of who God is and who we are meant to be. We can use the Bible to learn what is right and wrong. It teaches us how to walk through life and how to survive in hard times. It can help us know how to express gladness in good times. And best of all, it teaches us how to have a relationship with the God who loves us so much!

 Your word is a lamp to guide my feet and a light for my path. (Psalm 119:105)

Why do the stories in the Bible matter to you?

As you read through the Bible's stories, you might think, "What does this have to do with me?" The people in the Bible lived a long time ago, probably far across the world from where you live now, and had a totally different way of living. At first look, it may seem like you have nothing in common with the people and places you read about. But don't give up so quickly! Keep looking. These are stories about real, ordinary people in history who experienced God! The same God who loves you and me today. We study the Bible to learn more about our loving God and how we can better live to honor Him.

Since the Bible is the Word of God, it is full of truth. But sometimes the truth is buried below surface level, making it a bit tricky to understand! In this Bible study, we are going to roll up our sleeves and uncover amazing truth-treasures!

Have you ever found a buried treasure?

Imagine this: You've embarked on a hike through some woods near your neighborhood. You're stepping on the dried autumn leaves, and you hear *crunch, crackle, crackle, crunch*! But suddenly, you step and hear something more like a *crunch, crackle, thump*! You kick the leaves away and look below to discover that your trail has been interrupted by something smooth and solid. As you glance down, you realize you're standing on what looks to be the lid of a great big wooden chest! You get on your hands and knees and begin digging it out with your bare hands. It takes all your strength to lift it up, but wow, this chest looks oldddd! You pry its creaky lid open and the sun's light floods inside for the first time in who-knows-how-long. The stale smell of mildew rises from within the box as your eyes fall upon a note! The fragile letter is dated 50 years ago and was written by a girl who lived in the same neighborhood you live in. It's all about what life was like in your neighborhood 50 years ago! She writes about who lived in the neighborhood, their plans for the annual Fourth of July cookout, and then the best part—she writes about a hidden hiking trail. Apparently, it leads to the best views in all the forest!

You just uncovered a really cool look into the history of your neighborhood! Of course, you decide to find that hiking trail right away and follow it up to the highest point in the woods. Your legs are sore, but you keep climbing, and after a couple of forks in the road and lots of sweat, you discover a beautiful view of your neighborhood that you've never seen before!

The Bible is kind of like that letter. Yes, it's very old (thousands of years old, in fact!), but it's a wayyyy better treasure! It tells us the story of how God loves His people in this world and even helps us see things differently if we follow the trails of those who've lived and walked before us. There is so much we can learn from it and apply to our own lives.

How do we study the Bible?

At True Girl, we have developed a really cool way to study the Bible. We call it **the Four-Z Method of Bible Study**! All you have to do is:

ZOOM **ZOOM** ZERO **ZIP**!

We will teach you how to:

⭐ **ZOOM OUT**—get the big picture

⭐ **ZOOM IN**—understand the details

⭐ **ZERO IN**—find out what it really means

⭐ **ZIP IT**—learn what God wants you to do with it

Whew, that was fast! Let me explain it a bit more slowly.

The basics of Zooming— Who? What? Where? When? Why?

We'll be doing a lot of **ZOOMING**! That's when we understand the *who*, *what*, *when*, *where*, and *why*. Zooming is the most time-consuming part of Bible study. As you observe, you ask and answer a lot of questions. As we examine the life of Mary, I'll ask the questions, and you get to answer them. (We'll make this fun with quizzes, puzzles, and cool clues.) Sometimes we'll clearly be zooming out. And other times, we'll obviously be zooming in. But sometimes it's a big mixture of both at the same time.

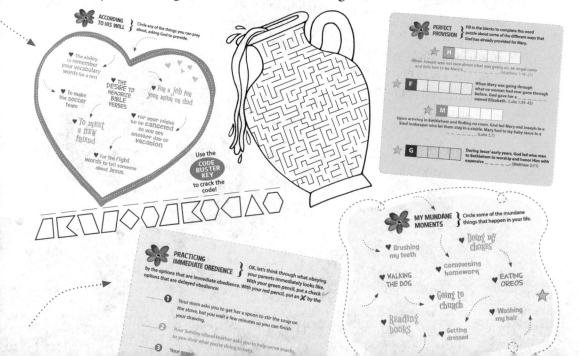

ZOOM OUT!

One way to get a better understanding of what the Bible means is to look at the *context*.

········► { **context:** the background of the story }

To see the context, we "zoom out" and look for what else was going on in the background. Our goal is to better understand the time, place, and people. It's kind of like hiking up that secret path to get a bird's-eye view of your neighborhood. We ask questions like:

- ★ **When** did this happen?
- ★ **Where** did it happen?
- ★ **Who** was there?
- ★ **What** else was happening at that time?
- ★ **Why** did God allow it in their lives?

The answers help us understand the story.

ZOOM IN!

Another way to gain a better understanding of what something in the Bible means for us is to look at the *particulars*.

········► { **particulars:** the details of the story }

To see the particulars, we dig deeper below the surface—like when you step on a treasure chest and lean down to uncover and lift it up! These details are more clearly seen when we "zoom in" on a word or a phrase to figure out what it really means.

This gets a little tricky when we're studying the Bible. Why? Well, did you know that the Bible wasn't originally written in English? The Bible has two parts—the Old Testament and the New Testament. Mary's story is found in the New Testament, which was mostly written in the ancient Greek language.

········► { **Greek:** the original language the New Testament was written in }

In Greek, some words have different meanings than they do in English. For instance, say I shout, "Heads up!" You probably know that means to "duck," and you would put your head down (not up). Well, if you translate that directly into another language, someone might actually lift their head high into the air. (And they might get hit with a baseball or something!)

Unless you understand the ancient Greek language and how it was used in the culture during this time, you won't understand everything you study about Mary. Let me give you an example. Once when Mary asked Jesus to do something, He said, "Woman, what does this have to do with me?" (John 2:4 ESV).

Hmmmmm! You might think, "Wow . . . that was so disrespectful! I'd be in so much trouble if I called my mom *WOMAN*!" BUT back then, in this specific culture, it was not a disrespectful way to greet your mom at all! On the contrary, it was a very respectful thing to call her a woman. When we zoom in on this word to understand the language and the people, we understand better what's happening in the story. (Now, let me give you a little friendly advice here—don't go around calling your mom "Woman!" You don't live in that ancient culture, so I don't think she'd appreciate it!)

As we study Mary, be prepared to zoom in on the particulars—including specific words—because we'll get a much clearer, close-up shot of what's happening in her story.

ZERO IN: What does it mean?

Once we've considered the *context* (by zooming out) and the *particulars* (by zooming in), we'll need to think a little harder to uncover *why* this story or truth is in the Bible. You're going to have the opportunity to ZERO IN, or focus on, what it might mean *for you*! Once again, I've got ya, True Girl! I'm going to help you do this with questions, and you'll get to fill in the answers.

ZIP IT UP: What does God want me to do with it?

To complete your study, you'll need to respond to God. After all, the Bible contains His words. So, when you read it . . . well, if you don't respond, that's kinda just like a one-sided conversation. During this study, you'll have the opportunity to obey, agree with, or even question God. (Sometimes it can feel wrong to question Him, but I promise that it's OK to ask God questions. He wants you to express your thoughts and feelings to Him.) At the end of every chapter you'll wrap up by talking to God about what you've learned. Then you can ask Him what to do with what you've discovered. You'll get to ZIP IT UP with God!

Welcome to the True Girl 4-Z Method of Bible study!

All of this zooming, zipping, and zeroing is really a fun way to enter into what's called the Inductive Method of Bible study. Some people use big, boring words to learn how to study the Bible, but I think it should be fun. So, my team and I reworked it and named it the 4-Z Method of Bible Study.

What you'll need

⭐ Your Bible (You won't use it a lot, but that's because I'm keeping this Bible study simple. All of the verses you'll need are printed right in this book. BUT, I want you to get in the habit of having your very own treasured Bible on hand and marking it up as you study!)

⭐ This copy of *Mary: Becoming a Girl of Faithfulness*

⭐ Some colored markers or pencils

Got it all? OK. Let's get those creative juices flowin' by using the 4-Z Method as we study the eventful life of an ordinary girl—Mary.

✳ What Is Faithfulness?

Imagine you are on a huge, long, super fantastic road trip. You have your headphones
and some new sunglasses. Your bestie loaned you her Travel Bingo game, Mom packed
all the delicious snacks, and your favorite True Girl water bottle is full of icy lemonade.
(Just don't drink too much! You have a looong ride, and your mom doesn't want to stop
every 30 minutes. You're gonna get to your destination if it's the last thing you do!)

As you drive through the super cool town of Ellicottville, New York, your
excitement builds. You cannot wait to see Niagara Falls! But it's still one hour away.
Suddenly, the unexpected happens. You lose the Global Positioning System (GPS)
signal. The car's GPS has just stopped working, and you have no map to rely on!
Today's super awesome digital maps are incredible, but they aren't foolproof.

You might think that things like your smartphone's GPS, Mom's personal hotspot,
or even your dad's super-dependable brain are "faithful." Although those things are
usually dependable, they sometimes fail. They cannot be relied upon on their own.

So, let's talk about *faithfulness*! Do you have any idea what it means? Take a second to think about it, and then write below your best guess of its meaning!

⟫⟶ _____

_____

_____

OK. Let's see if you're right!

What is faithfulness?

As we study the life of Mary, we'll discover that she was faithful. And we'll learn that we're supposed to be too. Here's a simple definition of the word:

> **{ faithful: able to be trusted or relied on }**

Being faithful to *someone* means you're a loyal friend, daughter, sister, or fellow student. Being faithful to a *task* means that you are committed to sticking with it, even when it's hard. The Bible says that God wants you to be faithful *to Him*. He wants you to be committed to Him so much that He can trust you and rely on you to choose His plan for your life.

The truth is . . . becoming a girl of faithfulness is super hard! None of us can be faithful without God's help. We do wrong things, go back on our word, and give up sometimes. We are humans, and we sin! Just like your dad's super-dependable brain, we are not foolproof.

The only reliable GPS in the universe

Thankfully that is *not* the end of the story! The Bible tells us that faithfulness is a fruit of the Spirit, meaning that it comes FROM the Spirit of God. When God is with us, He helps us to be faithful. We can rely on Him and use God's Positioning System, the only reliable GPS. (See what I did there?!)

Wait . . . so what is this super-dependable GPS, and where can you get one? I'm glad you asked. It's the Bible! The Bible can guide us through life so that we grow more and more faithful. You'll learn to be faithful as you read it and ask for wise advice from others who read it. It also helps if you talk to God a lot!

Here's one reason faithfulness can be complicated, though. It's not always going to be the great, big, ginormous things in your life that require faithfulness. (Like going on a mission trip with your family.) God gives you opportunities to join Him in His special work *all the time—EVERY DAY.* How you respond to the little, daily things matters a whole lot. (Like helping your mom do the dishes or being kind to your little bro!) Those small moments of faithfulness are a prettttty good way to tell if you're ready for the big things.

If you're a Christian, God *will* ask you to be faithful—all the time, every day!

And don't forget: He will be with you, helping you do it. **Because of Him, being a girl of faithfulness is possible!**

As you turn the pages of this book and learn about Mary, my prayer is that you'd be encouraged to rely more on Him and less on your own abilities. And may you be given the courage to step out in faith, even when it's hard. God has beautiful plans for your life.

So now, without further ado, let me introduce you to Mary, a girl of faithfulness! **Let's start zooming!**

Zoom In & Out—Who? What? Where? When? Why?

ZOOM OUT!

Before we learn about Mary, we need to *zoom out* to understand why we need to be faithful. And today, we're going to zoom WAYYYY out! Can you guess where we're going?

We're headed to the beginning of time!

The very first words in the Bible are: "In the beginning, God created the heavens and the earth" (Genesis 1:1). God has always existed. He created the sun, moon, sky, land, sea, plants, animals, and everything you see around you! This includes the best thing ever . . . *us!*

God is a fair God. So, He didn't create us to automatically love Him. Instead, He allowed us to choose if we would follow Him or our own sinful desires.

Let's pause right there! We need to clarify one thing—sin. What *is* sin?

········▶ { **sin:** doing what is wrong or not doing what is right according to God's rules[2] }

The first man and woman, Adam and Eve, were tempted by a snake, which was the devil in disguise. He told them to choose to follow their own sinful desires instead of trusting God's perfect plan. Sadly, Adam and Eve chose to sin. Because of that, there is a gap between humans and God. Sin separates us from Him.

Thankfully, that's not the end of the story. God had a plan. A super-ginormous plan to rescue the world! Here it is:

····▶ God's super-ginormous plan to rescue the world

Right after Adam and Eve sinned, God promised that one day a Savior would come and crush Satan—the ruler of all evil. Then, God kept reminding His special people—the Israelites—about this coming Savior. The Old Testament is full of prophecies about Him. Prophecies are statements from God about what will happen in the future. There are over 300 prophecies about the Savior in the Old Testament. These prophecies were signs that God's people could look for so that when the Savior came, they could be sure to know it was Him. God's people studied these announcements carefully and knew some of the things they could expect.

PROPHECY PUZZLE } Find the KEY WORDS in these prophecies or announcements about the Savior.

```
E  W  R  M  Y  M  M  T  T  G  N  O  K  R  T  Q  Z  L
N  J  M  S  N  H  D  W  J  Q  E  O  F  L  F  W  W  C
D  F  N  O  E  A  R  T  H  L  Y  F  A  T  H  E  R  V
O  Z  G  K  I  N  G  D  A  V  I  D  R  W  K  O  U  I
G  W  X  I  A  J  C  Z  C  L  B  Y  E  N  G  S  X  A
H  N  O  Y  J  E  U  W  Z  Z  B  B  Y  G  Z  K  J  T
I  S  G  M  C  B  E  T  H  L  E  H  E  M  Y  H  D  Q
Q  O  R  U  A  F  B  Q  U  R  F  W  Q  Q  N  P  N  S
Y  W  U  F  Y  N  X  M  M  I  R  A  C  L  E  S  T  I
Z  K  C  G  Q  S  X  V  U  J  D  P  A  A  M  A  Z  Y
Y  S  Z  R  Q  U  A  E  F  U  L  T  Q  C  B  H  F  R
C  T  M  R  I  H  P  K  Z  X  L  B  U  B  K  T  C  B
```

CLUES

He would crush the devil and have a mom (who is referred to as a **WOMAN**) (Genesis 3:15).

He would be born in the city of **BETHLEHEM** (Micah 5:2).

His great-great-great . . . and more greats . . . grandfather would be **KING DAVID** (Isaiah 9:6–7).

He would have an **EARTHLY FATHER** (Isaiah 7:14).

He would do lots of wonderful **MIRACLES** (Isaiah 35:5–6).

He would spend time in **EGYPT** (Hosea 11:1).

* For puzzle answers, look in the back of the book.

God had all of this planned out since the beginning. Why? Because He wanted to rescue us from sin and death.

Congratulations! That was your first zoom-out assignment! High five!

Now, let's *zoom in* to the first chapter of the book of Luke, where we meet our girl, Mary. She's a young teenager living in the town of Nazareth with a perfectly planned life. Little did she know she was a special part of God's super-ginormous, rescue-the-world plan!

ZOOM IN!

Now that you have some context, it's time to start learning about Mary. Here's something important to know: One of her great-great-great-great (and lots more greats) grandfathers was King David. (Sound familiar?) As a child, she would have grown up hearing the Old Testament read out loud and been taught to expect and pray for the Savior, who she knew would come from her family. Mary was aware that her family was special. But she probably never imagined that *she* would be the one to give birth to the baby who would rescue the world.

Mary lived at a time in history when some of the Jewish people were *especially* ready for the Savior to show up. That's because a big, powerful nation, called the Roman Empire, had taken over their special land. The Romans treated the Israelites terribly. The Israelites wanted someone to release them from their misery, and they knew the promise was that someday that special baby would be born!

Some of the Jewish people were waiting and watching *faithfully*!

There's something interesting about faithfulness. It comes in handy when you feel bad about life and are experiencing doubt. And as you'll see, when we first read about Mary in the Bible, she also was struggling with those things.

Now that you understand a little background context, it's time to start learning about faithfulness through Mary's example. Of course, we meet her in what we consider the Christmas story. Even though we think of it as sweet and peaceful, it wasn't exactly like that for Mary.

LUKE 1:26–38

As you read these Bible verses, use a blue pencil or marker to circle all the words that tell us how Mary felt about the news that she was going to be the mother of the Savior she grew up hearing about. (HINT: You'll find two words that describe her feelings in verse 29. And one word the angel uses to describe her in verse 30.)

26 In the sixth month of Elizabeth's pregnancy, God sent the angel Gabriel to Nazareth, a village in Galilee, 27 to a virgin named Mary.

She was engaged to be married to a man named Joseph, a descendant of King David. 28 Gabriel appeared to her and said, "Greetings, favored woman! The Lord is with you!" 29 Confused and disturbed, Mary tried to think what the angel could mean. 30 "Don't be afraid, Mary," the angel told her, "for you have found favor with God! 31 You will conceive and give birth to a son, and you will name him Jesus. 32 He will be very great and will be called the Son of the Most High. The Lord God will give him the throne of his ancestor David. 33 And he will reign over Israel forever; his Kingdom will never end!" 34 Mary asked the angel, "But how can this happen? I am a virgin." 35 The angel replied, "The Holy Spirit will come upon you, and the power of the Most High will overshadow you. So the baby to be born will be holy, and he will be called the Son of God. 36 What's more, your relative Elizabeth has become pregnant in her old age! People used to say she was barren, but she has conceived a son and is now in her sixth month. 37 For the word of God will never fail." 38 Mary responded, "I am the Lord's servant. May everything you have said about me come true." And then the angel left her.

Have you ever considered how Mary felt when the angel came to tell her she was going to be the mother of Jesus? She was *confused* (or unable to think clearly) and *disturbed* (or upset). And according to the angel, she looked *afraid*.

The angel had to tell her that what was happening was actually very good news for the world.

Look at the verses again. Find the word "Gabriel" used twice to describe the **truth** about Mary. Fill in the blanks below.

"Greetings, __ __ __ __ __ __ __ woman!"

"You have found __ __ __ __ __ with God!"

Mary had a dilemma. (That's what you call it when you have to choose between two things, and it's really, really hard.) Would she respond to this news according to her feelings, OR would she respond faithfully according to the truth of the situation?

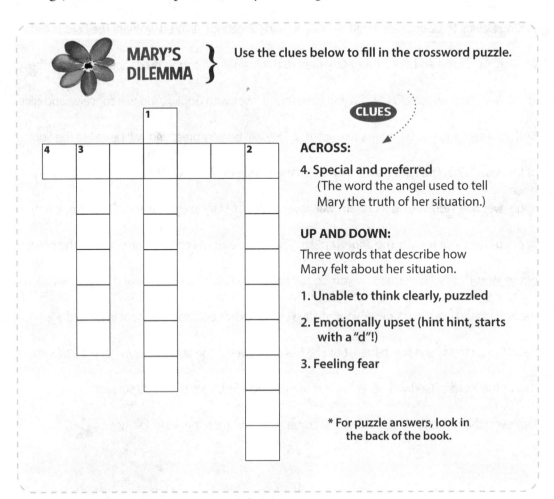

MARY'S DILEMMA } Use the clues below to fill in the crossword puzzle.

CLUES

ACROSS:

4. **Special and preferred**
   (The word the angel used to tell Mary the truth of her situation.)

UP AND DOWN:

Three words that describe how Mary felt about her situation.

1. **Unable to think clearly, puzzled**

2. **Emotionally upset (hint hint, starts with a "d"!)**

3. **Feeling fear**

* For puzzle answers, look in the back of the book.

Sooooo, let's review! An angel showed up to talk to Mary, and she felt *confused*, *disturbed*, and *afraid*. (To be honest, I would feel those things if an angel showed up to have a chat with me!) But the angel told her *not* to be afraid because God wanted her to be part of His special plan. Mary had to decide if she would trust her feelings *or* be faithful to what she knew about God and His super-ginormous plan to rescue the world.

Let's just consider how difficult this decision was for Mary. I mean, think about how shocking all of this must have been. Mary was just a teenager.

pause!

Does it sound a little strange that God picked someone so young to be the mother of Jesus? Let me clear one thing up. During the time that Mary lived, a teenager had reached adulthood. Twelve-year-old boys were considered men and had full-time jobs, while the girls were fully trained and prepared to start a family and care for a household. People typically didn't live as long in those days because they didn't have the medicine and knowledge that we have today. So, if someone lived to be 60, they were considered suuuper old. For this reason, adulthood started a lot younger! Does that make sense?

ok. UN-pause!

How did Mary respond to her dilemma? Did she trust her feelings? Or did she trust the truth the angel told her? Write your answer below. You might need to look back at Luke 1:38.

_____

_____

_____

Mary faithfully said, "I am the Lord's servant. May everything you say come true" (Luke 1:38). Today, we might just say, "Yes, Lord!"

Looking back, that seems like the obvious choice, right?! Mary had seen an angel with her own eyes, would get to be the mother of the long-awaited Savior, *and* was highly favored by God. But I don't think her choice was *that* easy. You see, Mary had part of her life already planned out!

Mary's special plan

Mary was engaged. She was planning to marry Joseph. They probably wanted to settle down in Nazareth, where they most likely would live the rest of their lives. Joseph would continue his work as a carpenter—building tables and chairs and boxes! And Mary would take care of the household. Eventually, after they were married, they would have children together.

But now, God was inviting her to be part of His super-ginormous plan. The angelic messenger invited her to become the mother of the Savior that the Israelites had been waiting for. God was going to use her to do something He hadn't done since the beginning of the universe. He was going to create life in a unique and unfamiliar way!

How did the angel tell Mary God intended to create this baby? Write your answer below. You might look at Luke 1:35, which we read earlier.

Just like Adam and Eve weren't created by a mother and a father, Jesus was not created by a mom *and* a dad! The Bible tells us that God intended to place life inside Mary's womb through His own supernatural powers. The Savior needed to be born this way so He would be fully God *and* fully man. Being fully God gave Him the power to defeat sin and death. Being fully man allowed Him to die in place of all men and women who ever sinned.

Mary accepted the invitation to be part of God's super-ginormous plan. She changed her plan to faithfully follow God's plan!

All of this made it suuuuper awkward for Joseph. It was hard for him to believe what the angel had told Mary because he'd never seen God do something like this before! So, God sent an angel to Joseph in a dream to explain the situation and to tell him it was all exactly as Mary had said. He wanted Joseph to marry the girl and be an earthly father to the baby. (Kind of like an adoptive dad!)

In the verse below, underline what Joseph did after the angel spoke to him in a dream.

 When Joseph woke up, he did as the angel of the Lord commanded and took Mary as his wife. (Matthew 1:24)

Wow! Immediately after God came to Joseph in a dream and told him the truth about this special child, he woke up and obeyed what God said—just like that! Joseph changed his plan to faithfully follow God's plans.

And this brings us to our very first lesson in faithfulness. Both Mary and Joseph had plans, but they knew that God's plans could be trusted more than their own.

FAITHFULNESS LESSON #1:
A faithful girl trusts in God's plan.

Fill in the blanks!
Faithfulness Lesson #1:

A faithful girl _____ in _____ _____.

Now turn back to the beginning of the book. Find the two pages that say "Faithfulness Lessons" at the top of the page. Beside #1, rewrite the sentence above.

Whenever I read Mary's and Joseph's stories, I'm inspired by how quickly they responded in *faithful* obedience to God's plan. But I don't think it was any easier for Mary to be faithful than it is for you or me to be. So, *how* did Mary (and Joseph) trust God and obey *immediately*?

Well, here is an important fact: *THEY* didn't do it alone! Let's look back, once more, to the story of the angel appearing to Mary.

Find the first words the angel spoke to Mary. They not only include the truth that she is **favored** but another realllly big piece of good news for Mary. Where was God when all this was happening?

 _____

_____

The angel greets Mary by saying, "Greetings, favored woman! **The Lord is with you!**" (Luke 1:28). Mary was able to trust God's plan because He helped her do it!

On our own, we cannot make good choices. Our sin impacts EVERYTHING— including our ability to make good decisions. In Romans 7, Paul, a strong man of God, wrote about how hard it was for him to make good decisions in his own strength. He wrote:

> I want to do what is right, but I can't. I want to do what is good, but I don't. I don't want to do what is wrong, but I do it anyway. (Romans 7:18b–19)

Have you ever felt like this? I know I have!

Maybe there was a time when you knew the right decision to make, but inside you, there was a tug-of-war battle trying to pull you toward the wrong decision. Think of a time like that in your life and write about it below:

 _____

_____

_____

_____

_____

_____

All of us would fail at faithfulness if we didn't rely on God to be with us! I'm so thankful that God was with Mary and that He was equipping her to make a faithful decision to trust His plan!

Whew! That was a ton of zooming! Now it's time to *zero in* and apply all of that info to *your* life, sweet girl.

ZERO IN: What does it mean?

Let's take a moment to think about the plans you have for your life. Maybe they are plans for next week's big birthday party or next year's soccer team. They could be plans to go to college one day or to marry a man and become a mother. In the box below, write or draw out your biggest dreams, goals, or hopes for the future! Include all the details!

Now, I'm going to ask you a question. It may be a little difficult to think about, so take a deep breath. Are you ready? Here it is . . .

What happens when the plans in your heart are not the same as God's plans?

Ugh! That's not very fun to think about, and honestly, the thought can be kinda scary. It's super easy to *talk* about saying "yes" to God and letting Him guide our path. But it's way harder to turn that belief into *action* when it means your plans will change.

Let's look to the Bible and hear the truth about God's plans for you. With a red pencil or marker, circle three good things about God's plan for you.

"For I know the plans I have for you," says the LORD.

"They are plans for good and not for disaster, to give you

a future and a hope." (Jeremiah 29:11)

Based on those three good things, what can you believe when God's plan for your life isn't what you had hoped?

God's very words promise that He has good plans for you, and when God makes a promise, He keeps it! After all, He *is* perfectly faithful!

But I bet there are still times when you're disappointed that your plans don't work out, aren't there? **You're not alone!** Every person in the whole wide world feels that way when their plans need to change to fit into God's plans. And sometimes we don't say, "Yes, Lord," like Mary did. I think one of the reasons we don't always respond well is because we don't really understand how big God is (and we think we're pretty smart). It's harder to trust God when we forget how good, powerful, and smart He really is. Here's a little brain picture that has helped me to trust God!

Puzzling piECES

Have you ever tried to do a puzzle? Let me ask that again: Have you ever tried to do a puzzle without seeing the cover picture on the box? I haven't! Putting together a puzzle without knowing how it should turn out would be soooo frustrating.

Our lives are kind of like 10,000-piece puzzles, and we don't have the cover picture to know how they should end up looking. We stare at the table of life's messy pieces and try to put our lives together the way *we* think is best. But really, we have no idea how our lives *should* be put together. Thankfully, God does! He knows all things because He *designed* the puzzle. God knows precisely what the finished product should look like.

Proverbs 3:5–6 tells us what to do when our plans get changed. Underline the action words below that tell you how to respond to God's plan.

> Trust in the LORD with all your heart; do not depend on your own understanding. Seek his will in all you do, and he will show you which path to take. (Proverbs 3:5–6)

God won't ever ask you to be the mother of His Son. There is only one Savior of the world, and He has already been born. But He *will* invite you to trust His plan. In fact, He wants you to seek it!

You aren't only supposed to trust God for the BIG things, though. God wants you to seek His way in "ALL YOU DO" (Proverbs 3:6). God knew that Mary and Joseph could be relied upon to do one of the most important missions ever assigned to humans—to take care of the Savior of the world when He was born and as He grew up. That was a BIG thing! How did God know this?

Well, besides the fact that He is God and knows everything, it's possible that He observed their lives. Of course, we don't know exactly what their lives were like before the angels came to tell them about their special role in God's plan. But we can guess that they were probably practicing faithfulness in the little things before God showed up with this big thing!

When I think about how Mary might have practiced faithfulness, I imagine she could have done these kinds of things:

♥ Cheerfully waking up early to help her mom get a head start on the day's chores

♥ Going to the temple regularly to hear the Old Testament read aloud

♥ Obediently helping her mom with little brothers and sisters, if she had any

What you do today matters! It's good practice for when God invites you to do something harder or bigger. Do you practice faithfulness in little things?

IN YOUR OWN LIFE

You make decisions every day that require faithfulness to God's plan. For example, read this verse.

 Children, obey your parents because you belong to the Lord, for this is the right thing to do. (Ephesians 6:1)

Today, obeying your parents is part of God's plan for your life. This verse is His invitation to you to participate in His plan. Are you saying, "Yes, Lord"?

FAITHFUL IN LITTLE THINGS }

You make decisions every day that require faithfulness to God's plan. Circle the things that you do to faithfully accept God's invitation to obey your mom and dad. Underline the ones you need to work on.

♥ Go to church **happily** with your parents (as opposed to grumbling)

♥ Respect the rules that your mom and dad make

♥ Do the **chores** your parents ask you to do **immediately** and with a **happy heart**

♥ TURN THE LIGHT OFF AND GO TO SLEEP WHEN YOUR PARENTS TELL YOU TO

♥ Trust that your parents love you and want to protect you when they say not to do something (it's usually in your best interest!)

♥ If you had to underline some of those, that's OK! All of us have areas where we need to work on our obedience to God and other authorities in our lives.

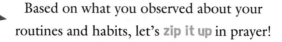

Based on what you observed about your
routines and habits, let's **zip it up** in prayer!

ZIP IT UP: What does God want me to do with it?

It's time to talk with God about everything you've learned. He can help you know
what you are supposed to do with it, my friend. I'd like you to take a few minutes and
sit quietly with God. Maybe say out loud, "Lord, how do You want me to practice
faithfulness?" Then, use the lines below to write down 3–5 ways you'd like to practice
faithfulness as you work on this Bible study.

_____

_____

_____

_____

_____

_____

_____

_____

_____

_____

_____

Now, since I've already got you writing, let's do a little bit more!

Sometimes, when we are studying the Bible, it's helpful to take notes and keep them
all in the same place. That way, you can look back later and see themes throughout the

whole story. At the beginning of this study, I created five special pages for your notes on the life of Mary. You've already written on one of them—the Faithfulness Lessons!

Turn to them now. On the first page, you'll see the three main characters in the life of Mary. Write their names under their pictures to help you remember who they are!

⭐ **Mary:** She's the biggest one in the center, labeled *The Mother of Jesus*.

⭐ **Joseph:** This is Mary's husband. He's the guy to the left of Mary.

⭐ **And, of course, Jesus:** You'll recognize Him as the 12-year-old to the right of Mary.

When you're done writing all of that down, come back here so I can say, "Goodbye!"

WOWOWOW! Talk about a journey! You just traveled over 2,000 years through the Bible. Good work, True girl!

In the next lesson, you and I will join Mary on the road *out* of Nazareth. After she heard this big news, she decided to take a trip. Where in the world could Mary be headed?!

A Faithful Girl Worships
When She Feels Like Whining

Imagine this: You're singing in your favorite spot—the shower, of course! After all, it has the *best* acoustics in the house. Plus, you can sing as loud as you want, and no one can hear you—at least that's what you thought.

As you walk downstairs, smelling like your fresh roses and cherry blossoms shower gel, your mom is sitting at the computer. You sit next to her and cuddle close, but then your heart drops as you look at the screen. In big black letters, you see the phrase "CHOIR AUDITIONS."

"Mom . . . what are you doing?" you ask.

"When you were singing in the shower, I heard that strong voice you have," she explains with a smile. "God gifted you with it for a reason, and I want to help you use it in a way that honors Him! So, I signed you up for choir auditions!"

What?! You do not like to sing in front of people! But you **know** that your mom won't take no for an answer. So, you decide to go along with it. Besides, you secretly think the idea sounds fun. Annnnnnd . . . if you're singing with a group, no one will be able to hear YOU, right?

Fast-forward to Christmas Eve!

You not only get into the choir, but you also get the star solo for the Christmas Eve service. People will definitely be able to hear your voice now!

On the day of the concert, a sick feeling of fear comes over you. You tell your mom. She says she understands why this could be scary and gives you a really good idea.

"Why don't you call Grandma Linda," she suggests. "I'm sure she'll have some good advice. After all, she sings in her church choir too!"

After three rings, Grandma Linda picks up.

"How's my favorite granddaughter doing?" she asks with a cheerful voice. (She can say you're her favorite because you're her ONLY granddaughter!)

You tell her how nervous you are, and she quietly listens as you share your fear.

"Wow! That does sound a little intimidating," says Grandma Linda after patiently listening to you pour it all out. "I understand completely. When I got assigned to sing my first solo, I was shakin' in my boots. I never wanted to be in front of everyone. In fact, I whined to the choir director. I told her I couldn't do it! But she helped me realize that God had given me my voice for a reason. I'll never forget what she told me."

"What?!" you ask, eager to hear some great advice.

"Maybe you should worship God instead of whining to me!" Grandma Linda giggled. "Yep! That's what she told me. So, I decided to have a worshipful attitude and sing to the best of my abilities, so that I could honor God with my voice. Choosing to worship instead of whine was the best decision I could have made."

Hearing this story feels like Grandma Linda is giving you one of her big, warm hugs right through the phone!

When you eventually step out onstage, you're pretty sure you'll still be a little nervous. But you are gonna choose to worship rather than whine!

It's time to learn Faithfulness Lesson #2, but let's review our first one. Go back to the Faithfulness Lessons pages at the beginning of this book. Find the Faithfulness Lesson #1 and write it below:

⭐ FAITHFULNESS LESSON #1: _____

_____

As we learned in the last chapter, an angel spoke to Mary and told her she was going to be a mother. The angel also reported that her cousin, Elizabeth, was six months pregnant. (This was incredibly surprising since she was wayyyy too old to have a baby!)

So now, it's finally time to catch up with Mary and see where she's going on her trip out of Nazareth! Let's start zooming!

Zoom In & Out—Who? What? Where? When? Why?

ZOOM OUT!

Read Luke 1:39 and draw a big star over where Mary was headed.

 A few days later Mary hurried to the hill country of Judea . . .
(Luke 1:39)

The hill country of Judea. Where is that? Well, Mary's journey started in her hometown of Nazareth and ended in a town called Hebron located in a part of Judea that had lots of hills.

Turn to the map that looks like this
in the front of your book.
Draw FOOTPRINTS from Nazareth to Hebron
to plot out Mary's road trip.

Do you know why I asked you to draw footprints? Because Mary probably walked from one place to the other. (Either that or she rode her faithful donkey!) Nazareth was 90 miles away from Hebron. It would take one and a half hours to drive that far in a car. So how long would it have taken Mary to **walk** it? Well, a human walks about two and a half miles an hour. So, if you're a math whiz, you might be able to figure this one out!

90 divided by 2.5 = _____

What if you're not a math whiz? Just take a guess.

Circle the length of time you think it took for Mary to walk to Hebron.

90 minutes   1 1/2 hours   8 hours   4 1/2 days

If you circled four and a half days, you are correct! At least, that's how long it took if she walked at a regular pace for eight hours each day. (My feet hurt just thinking about it!) Mary must have really wanted to go to Hebron. That's a big commitment. Let's find out *why* she went on this trip!

ZOOM IN!

LUKE 1:39–45

Grab a pink pencil or marker so, as you're reading, you can circle the name of the person Mary went to see!

39 A few days later Mary hurried to the hill country of Judea, to the town 40 where Zechariah lived. She entered the house and greeted Elizabeth. 41 At the sound of Mary's greeting, Elizabeth's child leaped within her, and Elizabeth was filled with the Holy Spirit. 42 Elizabeth gave a glad cry and exclaimed to Mary, "God has blessed you above all women, and your child is blessed. 43 Why am I so honored, that the mother of my Lord should visit me? 44 When I heard your greeting, the baby in my womb jumped for joy. 45 You are blessed because you believed that the Lord would do what he said."

Use that pink pencil or marker again and underline everything Elizabeth said to Mary.

I LOVE Mary's friendship with Elizabeth! We don't know for sure, but I think maybe Mary and Elizabeth had probably known each other for a long time because they were cousins.

What does the baby in Elizabeth's belly do when Mary arrives? And why?

➤ _____

_____

Where is God's Spirit according to these verses?

➤ _____

_____

Based on Luke 1:42–45, do you think that Elizabeth knew that Mary was going to be the mother of the Messiah? Why or why not?

➤ _____

_____

What does Elizabeth say about Mary's situation?

➤ _____

_____

OK, let's review. Do you remember how Mary felt when she first heard the news that she was going to be the mother of the Savior of the world? Circle the set of words that best describes her feelings.

Afraid and troubled   ❓   excited and happy

If you circled the first group of feelings, congrats! You got it! But remember, even though Mary was troubled and afraid, she still said, "Yes, Lord! I will be the mother of the Savior of the world."

Still, I have to wonder if Mary struggled with her emotions. I mean, she headed right out of town to see Elizabeth.

Here's a hard question: Why do **you** think Mary went to see Elizabeth?

_____

The Bible doesn't tell us specifically why Mary went to see Elizabeth, and because we weren't there, we can only make educated guesses. Here are some of my guesses!

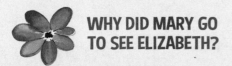

WHY DID MARY GO TO SEE ELIZABETH? } Put a star by the reasons Mary may have gone to see Elizabeth that you think are good ideas. Cross out any ideas that you think were not the reason.

To see if what the angel told her about Elizabeth was true because it would help her believe the rest of what the angel said

To possibly eat some delicious cucumber and melon salad—a favorite back in the day!

To take a worship lesson

To get some advice about her situation

To get encouragement because she felt afraid about what God was asking her to do

To go for a super long walk

* For puzzle answers, look in the back of the book.

Remember, these are only guesses about why Mary went to see Elizabeth. (We can't be sure, but I just wanted to get you thinking.) Let's see how Mary responded to her encouragement.

LUKE 1:46–55

Take a purple pencil or marker and draw music notes around this song. (Extra challenge: Instead of just reading these verses, make up a melody and sing it like Mary would have!)

46 Mary responded, "Oh, how my soul praises the Lord. 47 How my spirit rejoices in God my Savior! 48 For he took notice of his lowly servant girl, and from now on all generations will call me blessed.

49 For the Mighty One is holy, and he has done great things for me.

50 He shows mercy from generation to generation to all who fear him. *51* His mighty arm has

done tremendous things! He has scattered the proud and haughty ones. *52* He has brought

down princes from their thrones and exalted

the humble. *53* He has filled the hungry with

good things and sent the rich away with

empty hands. *54* He has helped his servant

Israel and remembered to be merciful.

55 For he made this promise to our

ancestors, to Abraham and his children

forever."

This song is so special it has a
name. We call it **The Magnificat**.
Magnificat means "magnify." And,
through this song, Mary *magnified*
God's name.

You've probably heard the word
magnify before! Write below what you think it means!

OK. Here's my definition.

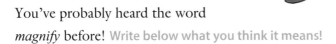

Wait, that doesn't sound right! Mary was *magnifying* God's name? I thought God was
already ginormous. Can we actually make Him bigger? Good question.

We magnify God's name like a telescope magnifies the moon! The moon is already huge and doesn't need to be bigger. But when we use a telescope to magnify it, we have help seeing the moon through our very limited human vision.

Magnifying God works the same way. There are some things we do that help us focus on who God is and see just how big He is—even though our understanding is limited. Worship is one of those things! It helps us put God in His proper perspective in our eyes. Through our worship, we draw close to Him and, as a result, can magnify His name to other people, making God's greatness more evident to them! Through Mary's worship, God was magnified.

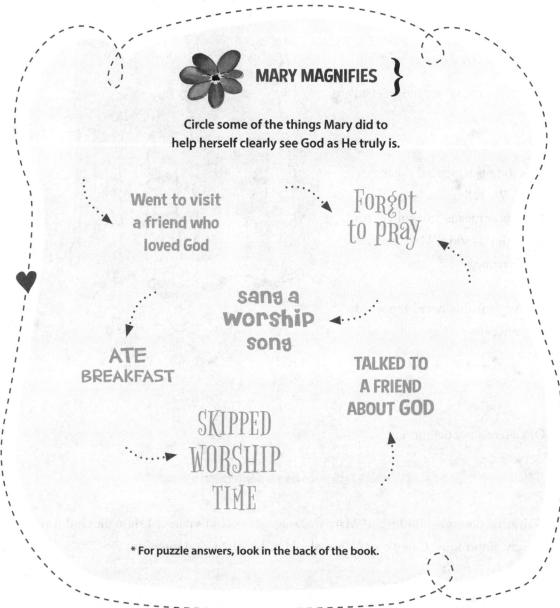

MARY MAGNIFIES }

Circle some of the things Mary did to
help herself clearly see God as He truly is.

Went to visit
a friend who
loved God

Forgot
to pray

sang a
worship
song

ATE
BREAKFAST

TALKED TO
A FRIEND
ABOUT GOD

SKIPPED
WORSHIP
TIME

* For puzzle answers, look in the back of the book.

You know, Mary didn't have to magnify God. She could have given in to her fear and troubled emotions. She had a choice in how she responded.

Using the pairs of words below, circle the one that Mary chose.

whine about the circumstances . . . . . **OR** . . . . **worship** God by magnifying His name

Mary magnified God's name by worshiping instead of whining, which brings us to

FAITHFULNESS LESSON #2:
A faithful girl worships when she feels like whining.

Fill in the blanks!
Faithfulness Lesson #2:

A faithful girl _____ when she feels like _____.

Turn to the front of the book and write "Faithfulness Lesson #2"
onto the pages where we are collecting all of your Faithfulness Lessons.
(You're gonna want to save these truth-treasures!)

ZERO IN: What does it mean?

Mary was not the only faithful follower of God who needed to decide if she would be a whiner or a worshiper! The Bible introduces us to lots of people who faced this dilemma.

You've probably heard of Abraham, right? Well, he chose to worship rather than whine when God gave him some land that wasn't very nice. It was rocky and didn't have any water to feed his animals and grow his plants. Do you know which land? **The hill country of Judea!** Abraham chose to worship instead of whine, and God eventually blessed him with the land he needed.

And remember King David? A prophet of God came to anoint him with oil and tell him that he was going to be the next king of Israel. But it ended up that David had to wait a superrrrr long time to become king and was running for his life during most of that wait. That's because the reigning king was super jealous. (Oh, guess what! That also happened in **the hill country of Judea**! Are you noticing a pattern?) David chose to worship rather than whine, and God eventually made him king.

Mary, Abraham, and David all had to choose to worship rather than whine when the things God asked of them were difficult. And the truth is, you'll face this same decision.

Unfortunately, whining often comes a litttttle more naturally than worship. Can you relate? *Here's the problem: Whining magnifies our problem instead of magnifying God.* (In other words, it makes our problems bigger instead of helping us see God's hugeness more clearly!)

Take a moment to look inside your own heart. Do difficult times squeeze out your bad attitudes and complaints, or do you choose to magnify God by having a worshipful attitude that demonstrates that you trust God? Draw a heart somewhere on the line below to represent how much you worship or whine.

whiner　　　　　　　　　A Little Of Both　　　　　　　　worshiper

I'm not asking you to plot yourself on that scale to "measure" you or make you feel bad about the times that you do whine. I just want to help you think about this: Do you worship or do you whine when you get squeezed by life's situations?

Do you think Elizabeth's encouraging words of truth helped Mary sing that Magnificat? Why or why not?

So, how can we be more worshipful and respond like Mary? I have two ideas based on what we just studied in the book of Luke. Let me help you see them.

IDEA #1: Find friends who help you worship by reminding you that God is good and He is in control.

Dannah & Janet

I have a friend who helps me worship. Her name is Janet. We have been friends for a long time and do a lot of cool things together. (In this picture, we were giving away free Christmas trees, hot cocoa, and kisses from goats as part of a church event!) Janet leads worship at my church, and I really like to sing loudly when she does. But that's not the only time Janet helps me worship God. When I am having a hard time, I sometimes talk to her about it. She gives me good advice that helps me remember to trust God and worship Him in how I respond.

Do you have a friend like Elizabeth or Janet? Someone you can talk to any time, and they will encourage you? (This doesn't have to be someone your age. In fact, it's great to look for someone older and wiser. Elizabeth was older than Mary! Your older, wiser friend could even be your mom!)

Draw a picture of your friend below. Write her name in the blank.

If you thought of someone who is like an Elizabeth in your life, spend lots of time with her. Who you are friends with has a huge impact on your life, because often you will become like the people you're surrounded by. If you're surrounded by whiners, you will probably learn to whine. But if your life is filled with worshipers, worshiping will become a lot more natural!

IDEA #2: Prepare your heart to worship when you feel like whining by knowing God's Word.

The next idea I have is a little harder to see in Mary's life. But, it seems logical that Mary prepared her heart to worship. Her worshipful spirit wasn't something she just woke up with one morning. She planned to be worshipful. How do I know this? Well, we don't know exactly what happened during Mary's early life, but we can see clues about what her life may have been like before she became the mother of Jesus. For example, every time Mary was asked to do something difficult, she spoke God's TRUTH and responded obediently. That doesn't just happen! She probably built this habit by knowing God's Word and living by what it said. Mary probably put these good habits into practice *before* she needed them, so that when pressing times came, she was *prepared* to worship instead of whine.

Here are some verses that I have meditated on to help me prepare my heart to worship. (*Meditate* just means I slow down and think about them carefully.) These verses are some of my favorite pieces of God's Word for puzzling times! Take an orange pencil or marker and circle the three things we are told to do ALL THE TIME no matter what!

 Always be joyful. Never stop praying. Be thankful in all circumstances, for this is God's will for you who belong to Christ Jesus.

(1 Thessalonians 5:16–18)

Use the same orange pencil or marker to underline why we should do those three things!

It is **God's will**. That means it is *His plan* for you to be joyful, to never stop being in communication with Him, and to be thankful. That's another way of saying: God wants you to worship instead of whine.

IN YOUR OWN LIFE

OK, let's bring it home. Think about something puzzling, troubling, or fearful that's going on in your life right now.

In the box on the left, draw a picture of what's challenging you. Then in the box on the right, imagine what worshiping God looks like in your situation.

Guess what?!
I have a little gift for you!

My friend Julia (who is the artist for this book) made the next page for you. It's a coloring page that will help you meditate on 1 Thessalonians 5:16–18. Do you see the little dotted line on it? **I want you to take some scissors and cut that page out—yes, you heard me right—**

Cut it out!

(This is probably the only time you'll ever get to cut a page out of a book, so enjoy it!)

After you've cut it out, take pens, pencils, markers, or paint—whatever kind of art supplies you like—and color, color, color! This is going to be your memory verse page for the rest of this Bible study! After you make it beautiful, I want you to hang it up on your bathroom mirror and say it during the time it takes to wash your hands. After a few weeks, you probably will have these verses memorized! Then, whenever you want to whine or complain, you can remember to be joyful, pray, and express thankfulness to God when you're tempted to whine!

So, go ahead, take some time to create, and then come back so we can zip it up!

Always Be Joyful
Never Stop
Praying
Be thankful in all circumstances,
for this is
God's Will
for you who belong to
Christ Jesus.

1 Thessalonians 5:16-18

ZIP IT UP: What does God want me to do with it?

You're back! Whoop, whoop! Before we both part ways and go about our day, I want to give you some time to write a prayer of worship to God. This prayer doesn't have to be complicated and fancy. If you want some ideas, here are a few ways that help me pray worshipfully. You could:

♥ Tell God something you love about Him, like His power or love

♥ Write one thing you are thankful for, like a soft bed to sleep in or yummy food to eat

♥ Praise God for the past ways He has worked in your life, like the time He healed you or provided money your family needed

God adores hearing you pray because He LOVES when His daughters want to talk with Him. Now, use the lines below to worship God.

Wow, I just loved spending time with you and Mary today. If you thought *this* was exciting, you'll love our next study session. Mary is going to need her worship! She, Joseph, and baby Jesus get into a dangerous situation with only one way out. The life of baby Jesus is in danger, but, thankfully, an angel comes again with another important message. And suddenly, Mary is on *another* road trip. But this time, it's not just a path to another city. It's a road out of the country.

✳ A Faithful Girl Is Immediately Obedient

Imagine this . . . you're in South Africa, and the weather is a perfect 75 degrees with a bit of wind. Starting tomorrow, you'll be having the time of your life seeing animals out in the wild that you'd normally only see at a zoo—giraffes, zebras, monkeys, warthogs, and so much more! You *really* hope to see what is known as the African Big Five: lions, leopards, elephants, rhinos, and Cape Buffalo. There is so much excitement bubbling within you that you have no idea how you'll sleep tonight!

You're staying at Hippo Hollow, a lovely place on the banks of the Sabie River. The website said that you'd see hippos while you eat dinner.

Only you didn't.

The sun is setting, and it looks like the only hippo you're gonna see is one on a picture postcard in the gift shop.

Super big, ginormous bummer!

Now, I told you to imagine this, but *I* don't have to. This really happened to me!

My husband, whom I affectionately call "Farmer Bob," and I really wanted to see some hippos.

"Let's go out for a walk," Farmer Bob told me and our two kids, Robby and Lexi. "We might find some hippos in the river!"

"No!" said Lexi. "We should *not* do that. It's *very* dangerous."

Despite her continued pleas, we set off into the African bush with nothing more than flashlights to guide the way and our new safari pith helmets to protect us.

We walked for a long time in the dark until we finally heard something! *Bubbles* *Gurgles*

"*What was that?*" I whispered.

Farmer Bob whipped out his flashlight and saw something! Right in front of us was a little sign that read:

BEWARE: HIPPOS AT NIGHT!

Ah! Our dream was coming true!

"*That must be the hippos we heard in the water*," I whispered what everyone else was thinking.

Lexi piped up again: "Did you *see* the sign? We should not be out here! Hippos are very dangerous."

But Farmer Bob and I did not listen because we could not control our excitement. Pushing through the brush, we suddenly saw tinyyyy ears flicking just above the water in the distance. Not one set, or two, or three, or even four . . . but FIVE hippos were right there in the water. I was tempted to run toward them! But, right at that moment, Lexi begged, "Let's go back, pleeaaaaaase!"

We decided to listen to her this time.

The next morning, we told our safari guide about our adventures, and his white toothy smile faded fast. Why was he suddenly so serious?

"That was not a good idea," he said. "Hippos are one of the most dangerous animals in the whole world. They can outrun humans and have one of the strongest jaws in all of the animal kingdom. If there had been babies out with those adults, you'd probably be dead."

I sat there, my heart and mind racing.

And then Lexi said, "We should have obeyed those signs!"

True enough, Lexi! True enough!

Now, enough about hippos.

Let's do a little Faithfulness Lesson refresher. Go back to the timeline at the beginning of this book and copy down our first two Faithfulness Lessons below:

⭐ **FAITHFULNESS LESSON #1** _____

_____

⭐ **FAITHFULNESS LESSON #2** _____

_____

_____

Fantastic!

Now, I have a few questions for ya. Have you been practicing faithfulness? Has it been hard or easy? Are you choosing to trust God's plan over your own? Have you been worshiping or whining?

Use the lines below to write about how putting faithfulness into practice is going!

➤ _____

_____

_____

_____

_____

If you're not doing too well with practicing faithfulness, that's OK. Don't be discouraged. Use the lines above to jot down ways you can remind yourself to faithfully trust and worship God.

Let's get started on today's new study adventure! When we last hung out, I told you Mary and Joseph had some big stuff happening and were about to head out on an international trip. We are gonna get to that soon, but first: Do you like to travel? I certainly do! I have gotten to travel all over the world in lots of different ways.

Me with Nancy DeMoss Wolgemuth, my friend and cohost of the Revive Our Hearts *podcast, in front of the True Girl Tour Bus. It's one of my favorite ways to travel.*

Of course, you know I've been to South Africa with my family to do some mission work and take a safari. (And look for hippos, of course!) We've also flown to China, where we adopted our second daughter, Autumn. (That was after our safari.) We have taken the subways in New York City and hired taxi drivers to take us through the Dominican Republic.

I've traveled by water on a cruise ship, walked to my friends' homes, taken buses in Europe, ridden a bike in France, and lived on the True Girl Tour Bus to cross America!

There are so many ways to get around!

What is your favorite way to travel? Write all the ways you have traveled below and circle your favorite. Cross out your least favorite.

Now, maybe you love *all* the ways to get around. Today, traveling can be so much fun. But we're going to have to zoom out to learn that it wasn't quite as glamorous (or fast) for Mary. Let's go!

Zoom In & Out—Who? What? Where? When? Why?

ZOOM OUT!

Back in Mary's day travel was dangerous, difficult, and disagreeable. People often traveled in big groups, called *caravans*. Caravans provided safety because there were thieves on the road. Robbers were less likely to harm people who stayed in a group.

Not only was traveling unsafe, it also was extremely hard and uncomfortable. There were no cars, comfy seats, or cup holders. Some people would have traveled on animals, like camels or donkeys. But most people walked—everywhere! In their open-toed sandals! Because of this, long trips could take weeks or months. And without cellphones, you couldn't just phone home and tell the people who loved you that you were safe. Or—*gulp!*—that you needed help, if the donkey "broke down"!

Traveling was risky business.

But, in spite of all of its dangers, Mary and Joseph still took a lot of road trips.

Turn to the map at the beginning of the book.

Maybe put a bookmark or something there like a colored pencil. We're going to come back to it a few times today.

Grab a black pencil or marker. You should recognize two of the locations on this map from last week's study. Use the lines below to write the names of two places Mary has already been!

Did you get them? Nazareth is the city Mary lived in and is where the angel Gabriel appeared to her. The hill country of Judea was the other! Do you remember that place? It's where Mary went to visit Elizabeth for three months.

OK, buckle up; it's time to *zoom in* to check out the next few stops on Mary's itinerary.

ZOOM IN!

LUKE 2:1–21

Read the Bible passage below. You'll probably find it super familiar! Use a purple pencil or marker to draw a squiggly line under every location you read about. Include cities, countries, and empires!

1 At that time the Roman emperor, Augustus, decreed that a census should be taken throughout the Roman Empire. 2 (This was the first census taken when Quirinius was governor of Syria.) 3 All returned to their own ancestral towns to register for this census. 4 And because Joseph was a descendant of King David, he had to go to Bethlehem in Judea, David's ancient home. He traveled there from the village of Nazareth in Galilee. 5 He took with him Mary, to whom he was engaged, who was now expecting a child. 6 And while they were there, the time came for her baby to be born. 7 She gave birth to her firstborn son. She wrapped him snugly in strips of cloth and laid him in a manger, because there was no lodging available for them. 8 That night there were shepherds staying in the fields nearby, guarding their flocks of sheep. 9 Suddenly, an angel of the Lord appeared among

Consecrated comics

Use Luke 2:1–21 to draw a comic strip of the key events in the amazing Christmas story. If you need help finding that many, reread the Bible passage or ask your mom for ideas about how to break it up. (Your first square can be used to draw Mary on a donkey with Joseph leading the way to Nazareth! Then, just go from there and tell the story. There's no exact way to do it.)

Mary and Joseph
travel to Bethlehem

them, and the radiance of the Lord's glory surrounded them. They were terrified, *10* but the angel

reassured them. "Don't be afraid!" he said. "I bring you good news that will bring great joy to all

people. *11* The Savior—yes, the Messiah, the Lord—has been born today in Bethlehem, the city of

David! *12* And you will recognize him by this sign: You will find a baby wrapped snugly in strips of

cloth, lying in a manger." *13* Suddenly, the angel was joined by a vast host of others—the armies

of heaven—praising God and saying, *14* "Glory to God in highest heaven, and peace on earth to

those with whom God is pleased." *15* When the angels had returned to heaven, the shepherds

said to each other, "Let's go to Bethlehem! Let's see this thing that has happened, which the Lord

has told us about." *16* They hurried to the village and found Mary and Joseph. And there was the

baby, lying in the manger. *17* After seeing him, the shepherds told everyone what had happened

and what the angel had said to them about this child. *18* All who heard the shepherds' story were

astonished, *19* but Mary kept all these things in her heart and thought about them often.

20 The shepherds went back to their flocks, glorifying and praising God for all they had heard and

seen. It was just as the angel had told them. *21* Eight days later, when the baby was circumcised,

he was named Jesus, the name given him by the angel even before he was conceived.

Pause! Turn back to the map because we've got another trip to add!
Draw a path from Nazareth to Bethlehem with your black pencil or marker.

MATTHEW 2:1–23

Now, read the next Bible passage. Once again, use a purple pencil or marker to draw a squiggly line under every location you read about. Include all those cities, countries, and empires!

1 Jesus was born in Bethlehem in Judea, during the reign of King Herod. About that time some wise men from eastern lands arrived in Jerusalem, asking, 2 "Where is the newborn king of the Jews? We saw his star as it rose, and we have come to worship him." 3 King Herod was deeply disturbed when he heard this, as was everyone in Jerusalem. 4 He called a meeting of the leading priests and teachers of religious law and asked, "Where is the Messiah supposed to be born?" 5 "In Bethlehem in Judea," they said, "for this is what the prophet wrote: 6 'And you, O Bethlehem in the land of Judah, are not least among the ruling cities of Judah, for a ruler will come from you who will be the shepherd for my people Israel.'" 7 Then Herod called for a private meeting with the wise men, and he learned from them the time when the star first appeared. 8 Then he told them, "Go to Bethlehem and search carefully for the child. And when you find him, come back and tell me so that I can go and worship him, too!" 9 After this interview the wise men went their way. And the star they had seen in the east guided them to Bethlehem. It went ahead of them and stopped over the place where the child was. 10 When they saw the star, they were filled with joy! 11 They entered the house and saw the child with his mother, Mary, and they bowed down and worshiped him. Then they opened their treasure chests and gave him gifts of gold, frankincense, and myrrh. 12 When it was time to leave, they returned to their own country by another route, for God had warned them in a dream not to return to Herod. 13 After the wise men were gone, an angel of the Lord appeared to Joseph in a dream. "Get up! Flee to Egypt with the child and his mother," the angel said. "Stay there until I tell you to return, because Herod is

going to search for the child to kill him." 14 That night Joseph left for Egypt with the child and

Mary, his mother, 15 and they stayed there until Herod's death. This fulfilled what the Lord had

spoken through the prophet: "I called my Son out of Egypt." 16 Herod was furious when he

realized that the wise men had outwitted him. He sent soldiers to kill all the boys in and around

Bethlehem who were two years old and under, based on the wise men's report of the star's

first appearance. 17 Herod's brutal action fulfilled what God had spoken through the prophet

Jeremiah: 18 "A cry was heard in Ramah—weeping and great mourning. Rachel weeps for her

children, refusing to be comforted, for they are dead." 19 When Herod died, an angel of the Lord

appeared in a dream to Joseph in Egypt. 20 "Get up!" the angel said. "Take the child

and his mother back to the land of Israel, because those who were trying to kill the child are

dead." 21 So Joseph got up and returned to the land of Israel with Jesus and his mother.

22 But when he learned that the new ruler of Judea was Herod's son Archelaus, he was afraid

to go there. Then, after being warned in a dream, he left for the region of Galilee. 23 So the

family went and lived in a town called Nazareth. This fulfilled what the prophets had said:

"He will be called a Nazarene."

Whoa! That was a lot of reading and you probably have a ton of purple squiggle lines all over your pages now! But before we focus in on Mary and Joseph's next road trip, let me ask you a few questions. Mary and Joseph weren't the only travelers in this Bible passage.

What caught the eyes of the wise men in this story?

And when they were following it, who did they meet to ask for directions?

After Jesus was born, a star caught the eye of some wise men who loved studying the skies. These men traveled to Jerusalem and asked King Herod for directions. They wanted to know where the newborn "King of the Jews" could be found.

How did King Herod react to this request?

_____

_____

Herod wanted to be the only king, so he created a sneaky plan. Herod told the wise men that when they found Jesus, they should come back and tell him where Jesus was. Although Herod said he also wanted to go worship the new king, we all know the truth! Herod just wanted to kill Jesus! But the wise men didn't know this. They went on their way and followed the star, which led them to Bethlehem, where they worshiped Jesus. They gave Him some expensive gifts, perfectly fit for a king.

Circle where the wise men went next:

⭐ **Back to tell Herod where they found baby Jesus**

⭐ **To the Dead Sea to take a picture of themselves floating in salt water**

⭐ **Home because they had been warned in a dream not to visit Herod**

⭐ **To Chick-fil-A for some peach milkshakes**

When the wise men left Jesus, they were warned in a dream not to return to Herod. So, they went a different way home. (As far as we know, peach milkshakes hadn't been invented yet, and vacationing near the Dead Sea wasn't a thing!)

Write about who comes to visit Joseph (and Mary) after the wise men. What did this visitor tell Joseph to do?

⤙⟶ _____

_____

As you can see, the story gets even crazier! While Mary and Joseph were sleeping, an angel appeared to Joseph in a dream and told him to get up and take Mary and baby Jesus to Egypt. The angel told him Herod was trying to find Jesus and kill Him.

OK, let's look at something super easy but super important. Use Matthew 2:14 (from the passage we just read) to fill in these two blanks.

_ _ _ _ _   _ _ _ _ _

Joseph left for Egypt with the child and Mary.

When did they do what the angel told them to do? That very night they left, and just in time too! When Herod found out that the wise men had outwitted him, he was furious and announced that every boy under the age of two had to be killed. Herod reallllly didn't want anyone else to be king!

Turn back to your map to add another road trip. Grab that black pencil or marker and draw a path from Bethlehem to Egypt!

Now, remember with me how hard travel was back in the day! It was not easy for Joseph and Mary to make a trip that far! And now they had a baby to take on that donkey of theirs. But, despite all of these difficulties, Joseph led his family in obeying God. He didn't ask questions or make excuses. He and Mary obeyed this message from God to go to Egypt IMMEDIATELY!

This brings us to our third Faithfulness Lesson! (How are we already on #3?!)

FAITHFULNESS LESSON #3:
A faithful girl is immediately obedient.

Fill in the blanks!
Faithfulness Lesson #3:

A faithful girl is _____   _____.

Go back to your Faithfulness Lessons page at the beginning
of this study. Beside #3, rewrite the sentence above.

OK, so after a while, Herod died and another angel appeared to Joseph telling him they could finallllyyy return. So, Mary, Joseph, and Jesus took yet another long journey back to their hometown—Nazareth.

Turn back to the map to add **yet another** road trip. Grab that black pencil or marker and draw a path from Egypt to Nazareth!

 ZERO IN: What does it mean?

Let's learn about the word *obedience*. It's one we use a lot, but what does it *really* mean?

····▶ { **obedience: doing what you are told immediately with a good attitude** }

Obeying isn't something anyone can make you do (although I've felt consequences for *not* obeying a time or two)! At the end of the day, obedience is a choice.

Mary (and Joseph) made the choice to obey multiple times according to the Bible. They obeyed even though they did not always have a complete picture of what God was asking them to do, and together they faithfully trusted God's plan and believed that He knew best.

God sometimes asks us to do things without telling us all of the details. In fact, that's happened to me recently. My husband and I live on a little farm. (See why I call him Farmer Bob?) I LOVE my barnyard animals. There are my spunky horses, Trigg and Truett. I also have four silly fainting goats, two peppy peacocks, a llama, and one very short donkey . . . in addition to a dog named Moose (no, he doesn't have antlers!). I call them all my fur babies. (Yes, I know some of them have feathers!)

A few years ago, during my prayer time, I began to have the feeling that God wanted me to do something difficult—really difficult. Whenever I prayed, I felt that God wanted Bob and me to sell our farm. This thought scared me *so much* because my farm felt like one of the most important parts of my world. *Who would buy our farm? What would we do with our animals? Where would we live? When was God wanting this to happen, and why?* Those were just a few of the questions racing through my mind.

Dannah & hER fainting goats

I told Farmer Bob, and he said we should pray about it together. We asked God to bring us a buyer, but we did not tell anyone about it, which is a crazy thing to do! People don't normally walk up to your front door and randomly say, "Hey! Can we buy your farm?" We even prayed about what price God would want us to sell the farm for and had an exact number picked out.

And guess what? Just a few weeks later, some people we knew came to us and asked to buy our farm. And they *even* offered to pay the *exact* amount we had been praying about! Wow! God is awesome! We prayed some more and felt like God wanted us to buy property to expand the Christian high school we lead called Grace Prep and create a ministry home for True Girl that we would call GraceWay Farm. (We'll even move my animals there for True Girls like you to visit!) During this time of prayer, we talked with many wise, godly people, and they also felt like this was also the right thing to do. It seems like our next move would have been to sell the farm, move out, and go where God was calling—the perfect happy ending to a story, right?

wrong.

We chickened out. Now, we didn't FULLY chicken out. We just decided that *we* weren't ready yet. Bob and I sat down with the people who wanted to buy our house and asked them to wait. In *our* minds, it made sense. *We* didn't have our new home built yet, and *our* plans hadn't all fallen into place. But that is where I think we went wrong. Notice I said *OUR* plans. We weren't trusting God enough to immediately obey.

OUCH! I'm pretty sure there will be some consequences.

God is probably going to ask you to do big things someday. Maybe this will be protecting a baby the way Mary and Joseph did. (Of course, that baby won't be the King of kings!) It could be God will prompt you to be a missionary and live far away from home. Or to become a politician who honors God's rules in our country. He might ask you to share the Truth about Jesus in a grocery store with someone you don't even know. (It happened to me once!) All of those are really hard things. You will not always want to do them, but you should. You have to obey God.

WHY? I'm glad you asked. You should know *why* we obey God. Of course, there's the obvious answer: He's God. He knows what's best for our lives! But check out this verse that reminds us of *another* reason to obey God.

Read the verse below and use a red pencil or marker to draw a heart over the word "love" each time you read it.

 Jesus replied, "All who love me will do what I say. My Father will

love them, and we will come and make our home with each of them."

(John 14:23)

Obedience shows God that we love Him.

Whoa! Little sentence. **Big thought.** Read it again.

How do you think your obedience could demonstrate that you love God?

 _____

_____

_____

When our relationship with Christ is sincere, there is evidence of it: love. We love Him. And He loves us. Loving relationships are marked by trust. When you trust someone, you respond to them as if you do. Our true trust in God's care for us causes us to respond to anything He asks of us with, "Yes, Lord! We obey!"

But knowing WHAT God says to obey can be tricky sometimes. I mean, when it comes to things that are written in the Bible, like the Ten Commandments, it's very clear what obedience *is* and what it *is not*. ("Thou shalt not lie" is pretty easy to understand, right?)

But when it comes to letting God lead your *specific* life— like whether to sing in the Christmas pageant or go see a friend for encouragement or to sell your farm—it can be tricky. (He doesn't often send angels to reveal His plans!) But you can get to know God's voice by reading your Bible. As it becomes more familiar to you, you will sense Him speaking to you as you pray. God's Spirit whispers to us in our hearts and directs us to do things.

For example, when one of my daughters was about 12 years old, she kept thinking of South Korea when she prayed. I told her that sometimes when God wants to communicate with us, it goes something like that. Our minds just keep thinking of a certain topic when we pray. So, I told her to talk to God about South Korea. She did. All summer long.

At the end of the summer, she went to camp for a week and met a cabin mate she liked a whole lot. Guess where she was from? South Korea! And do you know what else? During camp, my daughter observed that this girl did not know Jesus personally as her Lord and Savior. At camp, when she prayed, God was prompting her to talk about how to become a Christian. So, she obeyed the Lord! And on the last night of camp, that Korean cabin mate decided to become a Christian. How cool is that?! My daughter was, in fact, hearing from the Lord.

But learning to hear, understand, and obey God's voice doesn't just happen overnight. I'm still working on getting it right every time! But listening to your mom and dad is a good way to *practice* obeying God. (And it *is* obeying God since He tells us in His Word to do it.)

Ask for help
when obedience
gets confusing

I want to make one thing very clear. God has put people in authority over you to help lead you, BUT not everyone in authority above you is being led by God. Here's something you need to know: God will never ask you to do something that goes against what the Bible says. So, if someone ever tells you to do something that doesn't seem right or makes you feel uncomfortable, talk to a trusted adult so they can help you.

PRACTICING IMMEDIATE OBEDIENCE } OK, let's think through what obeying your parents immediately looks like. With your green pencil, put a check ✔ by the options that are immediate obedience. With your red pencil, put an ✖ by the options that are delayed obedience:

_____ **1** Your mom asks you to get her a spoon to stir the soup on the stove, but you wait a few minutes so you can finish your drawing.

_____ **2** Your Sunday school teacher asks you to help serve snacks, so you drop what you're doing to help.

_____ **3** Your grandma asks you to grab the mail for her, so you quickly reel in your fishing line and run to the mailbox.

_____ **4** Your friend's mom asks you to clean up because your dad is coming to get you, but you're having a really fun time playing. You decide to clean up later.

_____ **5** You're finishing a game with your sister, and your mom says you need to go to bed. But instead, you squish in one more game before heading to your room.

* For puzzle answers, look in the back of the book.

In some of these examples, you **ARE** *eventually* doing what you've been asked, but not every one of them is obedience. Are you able to tell why?

In options 1, 4, and 5 you *do* complete the task that's been asked of you. But you *delay* your response. Here's a hard truth . . . actually, I'm not just gonna give it to you! (I'm gonna make you work *hard* for it. See what I did there?!) Bust the secret code using the code key below to find out the "hard truth" I'm talkin' about.

Truth Teller?

Delayed obedience is just:

Use the
CODE BUSTER KEY
to crack the code!

— — — — — — — — — — — — —

⬜ a
◇ b
△ c
⬜ d
⬡ e
▷ f
▽ g
⊠ h
◁ i
▽ j
▷ k
▷ l
◿ m
◁ n
⬜ o
▽ p
▷ q
○ r
⬜ s
⬜ t
⋈ u
⋈ v
▷ w
◁ x
⬠ y
Σ z

Now, I have some good news! *Sometimes* when we delay, God graciously gives us a second chance to obey. My farm story doesn't end with me being disobedient. After quite a few months, Bob and I realized that we weren't trusting God. We went to see the people who wanted to buy our farm, but they had sadly decided to buy land to build their own farm. We apologized to them for not trusting God's plan and asked them to forgive us. (At the time of writing this Bible study, we were in the process of patiently waiting for God to bring us another buyer.) But we still believe God wants us to build a new home for True Girl and our other ministry work. This time we've decided that when God is ready, we will *choose* to obey IMMEDIATELY!

IN YOUR OWN LIFE

I don't know what God will ask you to do in the future, but let me promise you this: He has good plans for you. Don't just take that from me, though! Check out what the Bible says!

Use an orange pencil or marker to circle some of the good words God uses to describe His plan for you.

"For I know the plans I have for you," says the LORD.

"They are plans for good and not for disaster, to give you

a future and a hope." (Jeremiah 29:11)

Some of the things God leads you to do will feel uncomfortable. Some of them might even be super boring. But all of them matter.

Maybe, when you're older, God will want you to serve Him in places you never would have guessed! Egypt was probably not in Mary's plans. The people there did a lot of things that did not honor God, and they did not believe in the One True God. Mary probably never saw herself living in Egypt until God sent an angel telling Joseph, baby Jesus, and her to go there! It might be uncomfortable to be the only Christian who lives somewhere, but if God is calling you to do it . . . obey!

Perhaps God will ask you to live in a normal town while you work a typical job and diligently serve those around you. From what we know, Mary stayed in Nazareth for years after moving back home, just going about her daily business as a wife, mother, and friend. It might be uncomfortable to live a quiet life for God if you dream of something louder, but if God is calling you to do it . . . obey!

Maybe God will ask you to do something without telling you how it all works out, as He did with my farm. God told Joseph that he and Mary were to remain in Egypt "until I tell you to return" (Matthew 2:13). By obeying, they were committing days, months, or even years of their lives to obeying God. Until then, they had no idea what was next. It might be uncomfortable to be stuck "in between" what God has asked you to do and understanding why, but if God is calling you to do it . . . obey!

Or, maybe now you feel God asking you to do things that make you uncomfortable, like telling your neighbor about Jesus or being friends with the girl who sits alone. Just remember, uncomfortable is not bad. God often calls us to where we least expect, and that's just part of faithfully trusting and obeying!

 ZIP IT UP: What does God want me to do with it?

So, True Girl, obedience is difficult, but one thing has made it easier for me: loving Jesus. My love for Him grows when I spend time in His Word, getting to know Him and worshiping Him. (Kind of like your love for a friend grows when you spend time with her.)

Today, I want to encourage you to do something to grow your love for God. Write your own Magnificat! That's right! Just like Mary. (Remember that from the last chapter?)

Using Mary's Magnificat as an example, write a song to Jesus about all the things He has done for you and your family. Express your gratitude to Him. If you happen to be a musician, you can turn this into a song. If not, it'll just be an awesome worship poem.

Amen, True Girl! You are on your way to *immediate* obedience. Although we will never be perfect at obeying until we get to heaven, we sure can do our best to honor God.

Now, it's time for us to say, "Au revoir." (That's "goodbye" in French!) But before you leave, I want you to guess where Mary is the next time we hang out with her.

If you said, "On a trip," you win the prize! If you haven't noticed, Mary has been getting *a lot* of travel experience lately! But *this* time, she isn't headed to Egypt, Bethlehem, or Elizabeth's house. Mary is headed to the BIG city! And when we meet her on the road, she is *very* stressed out!

A Faithful Girl Is Content in the Magnificent or the Mundane

T ime to wake up, Sleepy Head!"

Your mom's sweet but annoying voice jars you awake. Rubbing your eyes, you roll over to grab five more minutes of sleep. But suddenly you remember: the Science Fair is today!

You jump out of bed. *This is the day you've been waiting for!*

You've just spent the last three looooong months of your life using the scientific method for the betterment of the entire dog kingdom! You've logged what feels like a million hours and have carefully observed your dog, Toby. At times it was super boring. But you now know what kind of music is most relaxing for "man's best friend!"

After playing endless tunes for Toby, your lengthy journal notes record which songs make him bark, jump, and spin. More importantly, you also know what makes him chill out! You're pretty sure you can trust the conclusion of your study. After all, you used the scientific method! You can't believe you present your project to the public . . . **TODAY**!

At school, people line up to see your work, read your poster board, and, of course, pet Toby. Your conclusion is right there in big, bold letters:

The best part of your display? You're using your dad's Bluetooth speaker to play Beethoven and Mozart for all the passersby! (That's probably why Toby is so chill about all the selfies people are taking with him.)

"Can I have your attention, please?" The voice of the school principal, Mr. Butters, echoes through the school gym. "Our fifth-grade science teacher, Mrs. Peanock, will now announce this year's science project winners." The room grows silent as your science teacher takes the stage.

"We'll begin with third place," she says, leaning into the mic. You hold your breath! "For an outstanding project that concluded in something very useful for many of us . . . congratulations to Toby and . . . !"

You have just won third place!

As you walk forward to accept the third-place ribbon, you remember the moments where Toby was acting up, when you had to keep repeating the same test over and over and over, and then that amazing moment when you realized what helped your furry friend doze off.

Your faithfulness through all of that slow and quiet work has led up to one magnificent moment!

Speaking of faithfulness, let's review. Do you remember what the word *faithful* means? (Turn back to chapter 1 and find the definition if you need a reminder!)

········▶ **Fill in the blanks!**

Faithful: able to be _____ or _____ on.

Fantastic! Now, turn back to your Faithfulness Lessons page at the beginning of the book and write down the truth-treasures you've gathered so far.

⭐ **FAITHFULNESS LESSON #1** _____

_____

⭐ **FAITHFULNESS LESSON #2** _____

_____

⭐ **FAITHFULNESS LESSON #3** _____

_____

⭐ **FAITHFULNESS LESSON #4** _____

_____

Awesome job! Let's start zooming.

➤ Zoom In & Out—Who? What? Where? When? Why?

ZOOM OUT!

If you have a relationship with Jesus, it is an amazing gift. God planned to give you that gift a long, long time ago—before you were even born. But remember: Sin came into the world through Adam and Eve. It totally got in the way of our ability to have a relationship with God.

Soooooo, God began to reveal the plan that one day a Savior would come and crush sin and death. Then, God kept giving clues about this Savior to His special people—the Israelites. Do you remember when we talked about that in an earlier lesson?

Circle the word we use to describe the clues about the Savior that we read in the Bible.

❓ predictions ❓ prophecies
❓ forecast-ifications ❓ suggestions

If you circled "prophecies," you are correct! They are statements from God about what will happen in the future. There are over 300 prophecies about Jesus Christ in the Old Testament. They were kind of like puzzle pieces. When all of them came together and happened in the life of one person, the people could know the Savior had come! Some of God's people studied these prophecies carefully. We're going to meet two of those people in today's lesson. But first, let's look at a few of the prophecies.

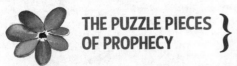

THE PUZZLE PIECES OF PROPHECY } On the left side are some prophecies about the Savior from the Old Testament. On the right side are records about Jesus' birth and life from the New Testament. Put the pieces of the puzzle together by matching them up correctly.

They knew He'd be born of a woman.
(Genesis 3:15)

God was Jesus' true father, not Joseph.
(Luke 1:34–35)

They knew He'd have an adoptive father.
(Isaiah 7:14)

He was raised in Nazareth.
(Matthew 2:23)

They knew where He'd be born.
(Micah 5:2)

Mary was from King David's family.
(Luke 3:23–38)

They knew He'd spend time in Egypt.
(Hosea 11:1)

Mary gave birth to Jesus.
(Matthew 1:20)

They knew He'd be called a Nazarene.
(Isaiah 11:1)

His parents hid Jesus here.
(Matthew 2:14–15)

They knew one of His great-great-grandfathers would be King David.
(Isaiah 9:6–7)

Jesus was born in Bethlehem.
(Luke 2:4–6)

* For puzzle answers, look in the back of the book.

OK, it's time to meet two of the people who studied those prophecies and were waiting with excitement for the Savior to show up!

ZOOM IN!

Have you ever been to a baby dedication service at church? It's a cool way for parents to promise to raise their child to know and love God! Well, Mary and Joseph did something like that. They wanted to dedicate baby Jesus to God. Let's read about it.

LUKE 2:22–38

Use a yellow pencil or marker to circle the name of the city where Mary and Joseph took Jesus for a special dedication. Also circle the building where they went. Then put squares around the names of the two special people who they meet in that special location.

22 Then it was time for their purification offering, as required by the law of Moses after the birth of a child; so his parents took him to Jerusalem to present him to the Lord. 23 The law of the Lord says, "If a woman's first child is a boy, he must be dedicated to the LORD." 24 So they offered the sacrifice required in the law of the Lord—"either a pair of turtledoves or two young pigeons." 25 At that time there was a man in Jerusalem named Simeon. He was righteous and devout and was eagerly waiting for the Messiah to come and rescue Israel. The Holy Spirit was upon him 26 and had revealed to him that he would not die until he had seen the Lord's Messiah. 27 That day the Spirit led him to the Temple. So when Mary and Joseph came to present the baby Jesus to the Lord as the law required, 28 Simeon was there. He took the child in his arms and praised God, saying, 29 "Sovereign Lord, now let your servant die in peace, as you have promised. 30 I have seen your salvation, 31 which you have prepared for all people. 32 He is a light to reveal God to the nations, and he is the glory of your people Israel!" 33 Jesus' parents were amazed at what was being said about him. 34 Then Simeon blessed them, and he said to Mary, the baby's mother, "This child is destined to cause many in Israel to fall, and many others to rise. He has been sent as a sign from God, but many will oppose him. 35 As a result, the deepest thoughts of many hearts

will be revealed. And a sword will pierce your very soul." **36** Anna, a prophet, was also there in the Temple. She was the daughter of Phanuel from the tribe of Asher, and she was very old. Her husband died when they had been married only seven years. **37** Then she lived as a widow to the age of eighty-four. She never left the Temple but stayed there day and night, worshiping God with fasting and prayer. **38** She came along just as Simeon was talking with Mary and Joseph, and she began praising God. She talked about the child to everyone who had been waiting expectantly for God to rescue Jerusalem.

PEOPLE AND PLACES

} OK, let's see if you found all the key people and two important places in Luke 2:22–38. Use the clues to figure out the name or place you're looking for and then find it in the word search. The last word you're looking for tells us what those people did when they recognized baby Jesus.

```
G  S  B  A  J  M  I  O  P  H  T  B
B  I  B  N  U  M  Y  H  E  V  B  F
H  M  A  U  S  U  P  P  L  Q  N  K
N  E  Q  N  S  O  F  J  W  H  H  I
K  O  J  E  R  U  S  A  L  E  M  I
V  N  I  O  P  R  A  I  S  E  D  I
U  Z  J  W  H  A  N  N  A  I  E  E
H  H  U  T  E  M  P  L  E  D  J  H
```

CLUES

1. They were in the city of J__ __ __ __ __ __ __ __ (Luke 2:22).
2. S__ __ __ __ __ was a righteous and devout man (Luke 2:25).
3. A__ __ __ was a very old prophetess (Luke 2:36).
4. These two old people met baby Jesus at the T__ __ __ __ __ (Luke 2:27, 37).
5. When they saw baby Jesus, they pr__ __ __ed God (Luke 2:28, 38).

* **For puzzle answers, look in the back of the book.**

Imagine walking into the temple with your little baby boy. This is your first time being a mom and everything is new! In the last year, an angel has appeared to you, you've seen your *very* old cousin have a miracle baby, and shepherds came looking for your baby when He was born. It's probably hard to wrap your mind around the fact that the child you gave birth to in a stable is the long-awaited Savior of the world! But then, you walk into the temple, and immediately your little tiny baby is recognized by two people as the Son of God. Whoa. What a Magnificent Moment!

FREEZE!
MAGNIFICENT MOMENT ALERT!

What is a **Magnificent Moment?**
I'm so glad you asked!
Magnificent Moments are
times in your life where
something truly special happens
and you have a sense that God
has planned it.

In the case of this story in the temple,
we don't have to wonder if God planned it!

Based on Luke 2:27, WHO told Simeon to go to the temple the same day that Mary and Joseph took Jesus to be dedicated to God? And WHAT did Simeon do when he realized the long-awaited Messiah—or Savior of the world—had finally come?

The Bible tells us that Mary and Joseph were *amazed* when they heard Simeon pray to God about their child. Then, one of my favorite parts of the story happens. Simeon turns to Mary and says something mysterious.

Go back to the Bible passage and use your pink pencil or marker to highlight what Simeon said to Mary.

What was Simeon doing? He was prophesying! God was using him to tell Mary some important things, including:

⭐ The fact that some people in Israel would not believe in Jesus

⭐ The sad truth that being the mother of Jesus was going to bring some hard, painful things into Mary's life (This was referring to Jesus' death.)

While Simeon is telling her this, Anna overhears him. And suddenly, she knows . . . the Savior has come! **Imagine!** As if one random person recognizing Jesus weren't crazy enough, another woman known for proclaiming the truth of God comes up and starts giving thanks to God! She knew the promised Savior had come and began that day to tell everyone she knew.

Talk about a baby dedication!

Pretend you are Mary. How would you feel as you walked out of the temple that day?

I can imagine Mary walked out of the temple, holding baby Jesus in her arms, feeling excitement and wonder in her heart. But there was another time Mary and Jesus came to the temple when he was older.

Let's keep reading in Luke 2.

We are going to need to fast-forward **12 long years**. Mary is living in the town of Nazareth with Joseph and Jesus. Each year, they celebrate the Passover feast. And guess what? This requires an annual road trip! Let's find out where they are heading. (They sure are frequent travelers, aren't they?!)

LUKE 2:41–52

Find the name of the city where they celebrated Passover and use your yellow pencil or marker to draw a triangle over it each time it appears.

41 Every year Jesus' parents went to Jerusalem for the Passover festival. **42** When Jesus was twelve years old, they attended the festival as usual. **43** After the celebration was over, they started home to Nazareth, but Jesus stayed behind in Jerusalem. His parents didn't miss him at first, **44** because they assumed he was among the other travelers. But when he didn't show up that evening, they started looking for him among their relatives and friends. **45** When they couldn't find him, they went back to Jerusalem to search for him there. **46** Three days later they finally discovered him in the Temple, sitting among the religious teachers, listening to them and asking questions. **47** All who heard him were amazed at his understanding and his answers. **48** His parents didn't know what to think. "Son," his mother said to him, "why have you done this to us? Your father and I have been frantic, searching for you everywhere." **49** "But why did you need to search?" he asked. "Didn't you know that I must be in my Father's house?" **50** But they didn't understand what he meant. **51** Then he returned to Nazareth with them and was obedient to them. And his mother stored all these things in her heart. **52** Jesus grew in wisdom and in stature and in favor with God and all the people.

This year's Passover trip doesn't go super smoothly, does it? What happened that had Mary all stressed out?

_____

_____

I cannot even imagine not being able to find one of my children on a road trip! Wouldn't your mom be frantic and panicky if she lost YOU? Well, that's exactly what happened to Mary! She and Joseph were on their way home from their annual trip, and all of a sudden, they looked around and could not find Jesus. Mary and Joseph headed back to Jerusalem to continue their search, but for *three long days* they were unable to locate their son.

Where did they find Jesus? And what did He say to them?

_____

_____

Jesus replied, as only the Son of God could, "Didn't you know that I must be in my Father's house?" (Luke 2:49). He gently reminded Mary and Joseph who He was and *still is* today: the Son of God and Savior of the world.

Pretend you are Mary again. How would respond to this experience at the temple? (Hint: We don't have to guess this time. Look at Luke 2:51.)

_____

_____

Some versions say that Mary "treasured" all these things in her heart. That means she was thinking about Jesus' words and actions and memorizing them so she could remember them for a realllly long time! They were special to her and she did not want to forget them.

It would take a lot for me to forget a day like that. Although it must have been stressful, it was also a **Magnificent Moment**.

ZERO IN: What does it mean?

The two temple scenes are some pretty Magnificent Moments in the life of Mary, Joseph, and Jesus. On a scale of 1 to 10, how magnificent do you think your life is?

My Magnificent Moments

1   2   3   4   5   6   7   8   9   10

"not at all"   "sometimes"   "100%—all the time!"

Do you wish your life were more magnificent? Why or why not?

_____

_____

Here's the thing: The two Magnificent Moment stories we read about Mary today have 12 long years between them.

Magnificent Moments Timeline

Circle the years 1 and 12 in the Magnificent Moments Timeline below.

1 2 3 4 5 6 7 8 9 10 11 12 13 14 15 16 17 18 19 20 21 22 23 24 25 26 27 28 29 30 31 32 33

Birth

Temple

First miracle

After what happened at the temple when He was 12, we don't read anything else about Mary and Jesus until He is 30 years old! That's 18 years!!! (You probably haven't even lived that long yet!) After that, He had a lot of Magnificent Moments before He died.

Circle 30–33 in the Magnificent Moments Timeline. Then, take a moment and look at all those un-magnificent years in between!

I wonder how all of the years in between the Magnificent Moments looked. *What were Mary's typical days like? How did she spend her time? Was the rest of her life as exciting as these Magnificent Moments?*

Probably not.

Here's what we do know: Mary and her family continued to live in Nazareth. Most women who lived there back then spent their days doing some pretty ordinary things. Their mission in life was to keep the family fed and the home functioning.

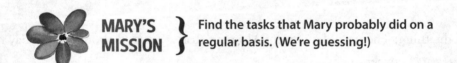

MARY'S MISSION } Find the tasks that Mary probably did on a regular basis. (We're guessing!)

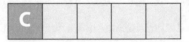

What she probably did when her house got dirty.

What she probably did when everyone was hungry.

What she probably did most of the day after she had babies.

* For puzzle answers, look in the back of the book.

Mary worked hard! And she didn't have all the modern stuff your mom does. For example, she could not turn the water on to fill a pot. She had to walk to a river or water well to fill jugs. And then she had to carry them home. And cooking was much different. She might have spent two hours a day grinding grain to make flour so she could make bread.

None of these things were magnificent. In fact, they were quite *mundane*.

What does that word mean?

··········▶ { **mundane:** lacking interest and excitement, dull, not special }

We all have a lot of Mundane Moments in our lives! For example, I love writing books and speaking at True Girl live events. But a lot of my time is spent in pretty boring meetings, organizing timelines for projects, and doing other mundane tasks. At home, my Mundane Moments include washing the dishes after dinner and ordering all the different foods for our farm animals. No one would see these parts of my life and think: *Wow! That's magnificent!*

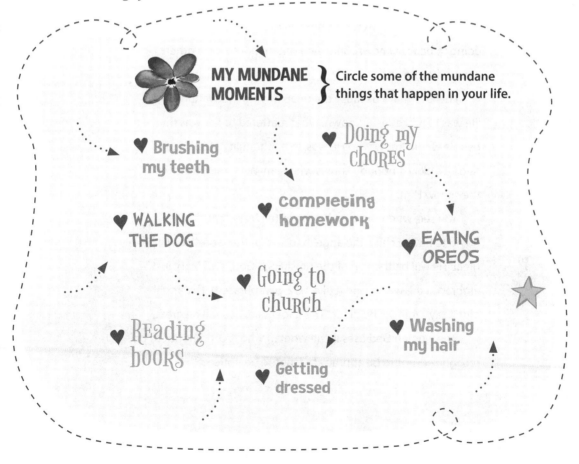

MY MUNDANE MOMENTS } Circle some of the mundane things that happen in your life.

♥ Brushing my teeth

♥ Doing my chores

♥ WALKING THE DOG

♥ completing homework

♥ EATING OREOS

♥ Going to church

♥ Reading books

♥ Washing my hair

♥ Getting dressed

I've noticed that a lot of the things we consider mundane are things no one sees. Think about how much of Mary's life no one saw! A lot of it. I want you to read something that my friend Nancy DeMoss Wolgemuth said when she was teaching about Mary's life.

Nancy on Mary

It's interesting to me that very little is said of Mary in Scripture after the birth of the Lord Jesus, and that suggests to me that she was content to be in the background. She was content not to be a well-known woman. Now, she's well known to us today, but she didn't know that she was going to be well known. She was content not to have others know who she was.

I believe that's because the deep driving motivation of her life was to make Jesus known. What mattered to her was that people would know who He was. In her humility of spirit, she said, "It's okay if nobody knows who I am. What matters is that they know Him."

You see, when the angel came to tell Mary that she was going to have a child, the angel had said of that Son, "He will be great. He will be the Son of the Most High God," and Mary just embraced the will of God (Luke 1:32, paraphrased). The angel didn't say, "You will be great." The angel said, "He will be great."

The woman God uses is the woman who is content not to be recognized, not to be appreciated, not to be noticed.[3]

It sometimes feels bad not to be noticed, doesn't it? Most of us desire to live in lots of Magnificent Moments, but God wants us to also embrace the Mundane Moments. Just like Mary did!

Do you know who sees when no one else does? God sees everything and He cares about our hearts in it all. From when we hop up onstage or win third place at the Science Fair to the long hours of playing music for your dog and taking notes on his response. From the Magnificent to the Mundane Moments in life, God sees it all and cares about it all. *What is He looking for? What does He care most about?* I'm glad you asked!

Use a red pencil or marker to draw a heart around all the things God sees and knows. You should be able to find six or seven things:

O LORD, you have examined my heart and know everything about me.

You know when I sit down or stand up. You know my thoughts even

when I'm far away. You see me when I travel and when I rest at home.

You know everything I do. You know what I am going to say even before

I say it, LORD. (Psalm 139:1–4)

God cares about our hearts and our thoughts and all the things going on inside of us! A lot of the things you just put hearts on are . . . well, pretty mundane. God sees them! Do you know why He notices them? The mundane parts of your life reveal your true heart. Any of us can have a good attitude when something magnificent is happening! For example, it's a lot easier for me to be kind, loving, and positive when I'm onstage at a True Girl show. But it's a whole different thing to be happy, loving, and positive when I'm mucking the horses' stalls alone. I've often said, "Who I am alone means more than who I am in public!"

This brings us to **FAITHFULNESS LESSON #4:**
A faithful girl is content in the magnificent or the mundane.

Fill in the blanks!
Faithfulness Lesson #4:

A faithful girl is _____ in the _____

or the _____.

Go back to your **Faithfulness Lessons** page at the beginning of this study.
Beside #4, rewrite the sentence above.

IN YOUR OWN LIFE

Earlier you considered some of the mundane parts of your life. Be honest with yourself.
What kind of attitude do you normally have when no one is around or when you're doing
ordinary jobs?

The next time you're doing something boring and tempted to have a discontented
heart, remember: The mundane prepares us for the magnificent. Mary was only
prepared for the Magnificent Moments in her life because she had been faithful and
content in the mundane. Now, she most certainly was not perfect, and I'm sure she did
struggle with discontentment sometimes because she was just a human, but there is still
a lot we can learn from her example.

I want you to know that although we're studying some of Mary's most Magnificent
Moments during this Bible study, the majority of her life we have no record of. It was not
magnificent, and yet, she was faithful in contentment to follow God's plan for her life.

Wait, I need to tell you what it means to be *content*!

·······▶ { **content: being satisfied** }

How do you think you can be content or satisfied in your mundane, daily activities?

➤ _____

There is no specific "recipe for contentment," but something throughout the stories of Mary's life struck me. Maybe you've noticed that after a Magnificent Moment in Mary's life, the Bible says Mary "kept all of these things in her heart and thought about them often" (Luke 2:19). Hmmmm. I wonder if she did that more than once. It seems possible that Mary meditated on Magnificent Moments during the mundane. I want us to learn to do that! So, before we finish today, let's **zip it up**!

ZIP IT UP: What does God want me to do with it?

I want you to spend some quiet time alone doing a little project. Often, in the Old Testament when God moved magnificently in the lives of His people, they would take big stones and pile them up as a monument. These rocks would stand as a reminder of God's faithfulness, so that during their mundane days, they could remember God's magnificence.

Magnificent memory monument!

Ask your mom if you can go outside and find some rocks! (If you can't find any and want to go buy some, there are usually rocks in the fish-tank section!) After collecting your rocks, grab a marker. Take a moment and think about the Magnificent Moments in your life. How can you tell if a moment is magnificent? Good question! You can tell if a moment was magnificent by two things: if it was out of the ordinary and if it was from God.

Think of as many moments as you can! Then, choose one word to describe each moment. Finally, write each word on a rock.

Afterward, stack your rocks up in a pile somewhere—maybe in a flower garden or on your dresser. Anytime you see that pile of rocks, you can be reminded of what God has done in your Magnificent Moments (Joshua 4:6).

(P.S. If your mom wants you to stay indoors, or you don't have any rocks, never fear! Instead of building a real monument, use the lines below to write about God's monumental Magnificent Moments in your life.)

_____

_____

_____

_____

_____

_____

_____

_____

That was special, True Girl.

If I could have you take one thing away from our time together today, it would be this: **In the magnificent and the mundane, your heart should stay the same.**

Now, I've told you some pretty magnificent stories today, but after the story of Jesus in the temple at 12 years old, the Bible is silent about Mary's life for many, many years. The next time we hang out, our girl Mary is quite a bit older. I can imagine that she's been storing these Magnificent Moments in her heart for years. Then, all of a sudden, the Bible brings us back into her life for what *I* would say is one of the most monumental moments of Mary's life. Mary's years of silence are interrupted by something miraculous! We'll learn about it next time!

✳ A Faithful Girl Believes God Will Provide

We can't eat these!" An entire group of teenagers held out their peanut butter and jelly sandwiches toward me.

I was in Zambia, Africa, on a Grace Prep High School mission trip with almost twenty high school students. That day we were helping a family who lived in a very poor village rebuild their home. But *all* the children who lived nearby gathered around as we worked. So a lot of our time was spent playing with them.

When the noonday sun was right above our heads we decided to head back to our van and break for lunch. All we had were peanut butter and jelly sandwiches, some bananas, and bottles of water. But we were very hungry, so I was sure they would hit the spot!

Apparently, the high schoolers didn't think so.

"What? Why can't you eat your sandwiches?!" I asked.

"We want to give them to the children in the village," said one teen boy. "They are starving and need it more than we do."

I thought this was a great idea, buttttt I had promised their parents I would take care of them, and not feeding them would be doing *the opposite* of taking care of them. Plus, there were only *twenty* students and there were *dozens* of children playing outside—all of them eyeing the van in hopes that we'd come back out and play.

"There will never be enough food for all of them!" I told the students.

Then, they said something to me that I will never forget. "Where is your faith? God will provide."

After some back-and-forth, I decided that if they would eat half of their sandwiches so I could keep my promise to their parents, we would give the remaining halves to the children. We broke those half-sandwiches into even smaller pieces and began to hand them out. My heart couldn't help but break at the thought of running out—even if every child took just one bite, there wouldn't be enough. I had no idea how this was going to work out.

But that day, I saw God provide as I'd never imagined.

Those starving children ate the sandwiches my students gave them, and before I knew it, I was looking at dozens of satisfied faces—mouths messy with peanut butter and jelly. Not only did they each get a bite—*every single one* of the children ate until their stomachs were full. Afterward, they handed the crust back. We collected the crusts and could not believe how much was left over!

That was the day I truly realized the powerful provision of our God. And it reminded me of that story in the Bible where Jesus fed a crowd of people with just two loaves of bread and five fish. The disciples collected leftovers and found there was more than when they started!

Before we talk more about God's provision in our lives, I want to review!

Try to think back and remember our previous Faithfulness Lessons. If you can, write them from memory, but if you can't, no worries, True Girl! Just turn back to your handy-dandy Faithfulness Lessons page in the front of your book and copy them below:

⭐ **FAITHFULNESS LESSON #1** _____

_____

⭐ **FAITHFULNESS LESSON #2** _____

_____

⭐ **FAITHFULNESS LESSON #3** _____

_____

⭐ **FAITHFULNESS LESSON #4** _____

_____

Lovely work!

Zoom In & Out—Who? What? Where? When? Why?

ZOOM OUT!

Now, before we hop back into Mary's life, let's get one thing clear. Ultimately, the most faithful One in this study isn't Mary. It's God! Remember, we are not able to be faithful without His help. Let's take a moment to remember many of the ways God has provided for Mary up until this point. God never left Mary stranded or abandoned, and it's important to remember *His* faithfulness. So, let's *zoom out* and remember God's provision in Mary's life until now.

PERFECT PROVISION } Fill in the blanks to complete this word puzzle about some of the different ways that God has already provided for Mary.

H ☐ ☐ ☐ ☐ ☐ ☐

When Joseph was not sure about what was going on, an angel came and told him to be Mary's __ __ __ __ __ __ __. (Matthew 1:18–25)

F ☐ ☐ ☐ ☐ ☐

When Mary was going through what no woman had ever gone through before, God gave her a __ __ __ __ __ __ named Elizabeth. (Luke 1:39–45)

M ☐ ☐ ☐ ☐ ☐

Upon arriving in Bethlehem and finding no room, God led Mary and Joseph to a kind innkeeper who let them stay in a stable. Mary had to lay baby Jesus in a __ __ __ __ __ __. (Luke 2:7)

G ☐ ☐ ☐ ☐

During Jesus' early years, God led wise men to Bethlehem to worship and honor Him with expensive __ __ __ __ __. (Matthew 2:11)

Of course, these are just a few of the ways God provided for Mary. There were tons of other things God did to take care of her needs.

God **always** provides for His plan. From the time the angel appeared to her, we see that Mary had faith that God would provide. You'll see how confident she was of that as we study the next snapshot of her life. Let's zoom in.

ZOOM IN!

JOHN 2:1–12

Uh-oh! Mary and Jesus are at a wedding and there's a problem! Use a red pencil or marker to circle what went wrong.

1 The next day there was a wedding celebration in the village of Cana in Galilee. Jesus' mother was there, 2 and Jesus and his disciples were also invited to the celebration. 3 The wine supply ran out during the festivities, so Jesus' mother told him, "They have no more wine."

4 "Dear woman, that's not our problem," Jesus replied. "My time has not yet come." 5 But his mother told the servants, "Do whatever he tells you." 6 Standing nearby were six stone water jars, used for Jewish ceremonial washing. Each could hold twenty to thirty gallons. 7 Jesus told the servants, "Fill the jars with water." When the jars had been filled, 8 he said, "Now dip some out, and take it to the master of ceremonies." So the servants followed his instructions. 9 When the master of ceremonies tasted the water that was now wine, not knowing where it had come from (though, of course, the servants knew), he called the bridegroom over. 10 "A host always serves the best wine first," he said. "Then, when everyone has had a lot to drink, he brings out the less expensive wine. But you have kept the best until now!" 11 This miraculous sign at Cana in Galilee was the first time Jesus revealed his glory. And his disciples believed in him. 12 After the wedding he went to Capernaum for a few days with his mother, his brothers, and his disciples.

Bible-times weddings often lasted dayssss!!! (Yes, you heard me, DAYS.) This meant the family had to prepare *lots* of food and drinks for the guests. In that culture, running out of food was considered irresponsible.

And the wine was running out!

Mary would have known that if this happened, the family might get a bad reputation. She wanted Jesus to solve the problem. She didn't ask Him to fix it. She just told Him about it.

When I first read about this wedding, I was surprised that Mary went *straight* to Jesus. Now, you might think, "That's obvious! Why wouldn't she go to the Son of God for help?" Well, it's a little more complicated than that.

What did Jesus say when Mary told Him the wine was gone?

 _____

_____

Jesus hadn't been doing miracles out in public for people to see yet. To remind her of this, He said, "My time has not yet come" (John 2:4). He meant that it wasn't God's will for Him to be revealed to the world yet.

What did Jesus do even though He told Mary, "My time has not yet come"?

 _____

_____

Even though it was not time for Jesus' ministry to be made public, He turned water into wine. This could appear to be a problem since God still wanted His power to remain a secret. But don't think that for too long. Let me show you something!

WATER INTO WINE }

Jesus used six jugs that were nearby to turn water into wine. Use a red pencil or marker to trace the maze. Begin at "water" and end at "wine."

WINE

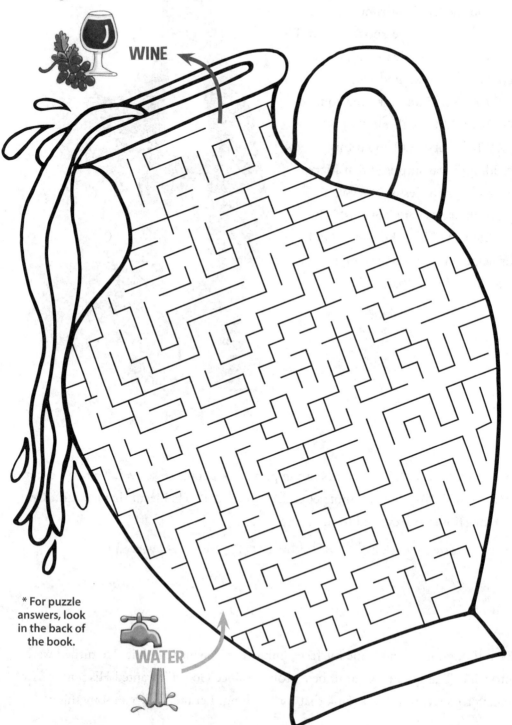

WATER

* For puzzle answers, look in the back of the book.

Look back at John 2:9. When the master of ceremonies tasted the water that was now wine, did he know where it came from? Circle one.

? no, but the servants did. **?** yes, totally!

? no one knew where it came from. **?**

Only Mary and the servants knew what happened behind the scenes of this miracle. And according to verse 11, Jesus' disciples knew where the wine came from, but the rest of this amazing miracle remained a secret. So, Jesus was not revealed to the public yet. God's will did not change when Jesus turned water into wine. And let me tell you, it was not ordinary wine.

According to verse 10, how did the wine taste?

_____

_____

In those days, it was normal to bring the best wine out at the *beginning* of the wedding . . . not the end! But the wine Jesus miraculously created was the most delicious at the wedding. How sweet of Him to provide what the guests wanted and to make it so yummy!

WHY?! Why did Jesus make this wine for the guests?

Jesus turned water into wine for ordinary people because He cared. That is our Jesus. He cares about the little things that matter to us, so He provides.

But there is another wonderful reason He provided. Mary asked. Mary trusted Jesus before she ever saw Him do a miracle in public because she knew who He was. That was enough.

This brings us to our **FAITHFULNESS LESSON #5:**
A faithful girl believes God will provide.

Fill in the blanks!
Faithfulness Lesson #5:

A faithful girl _____

_____ will _____.

Go to the **Faithfulness Lessons** page at the beginning of
your study. Beside #5, rewrite the sentence above.

ZERO IN: What does it mean?

Just like Mary came to Jesus and asked Him to provide, you and I can do the same thing!
Read the verse below and use a blue pencil or marker to circle the word *confidence*. Double
underline the words "according to his will."

> This is the confidence we have in approaching God: that if we
>
> ask anything according to his will, he hears us. And if we know
>
> that he hears us—whatever we ask—we know that we have
>
> what we asked of him. (1 John 5:14–15 NIV)

Now, this verse kinda makes God sound like a vending machine—like we will get
whatever we ask for from Him. But we need to note something super-duper-important
to understanding what this verse *actually* means! This verse says we will get whatever we
ask of God . . . **according to His will**. *HIS* WILL. That is the key.

What do you think it means to ask God for something "according to His will"?

_____

God's will is the thing that God knows is best for us. He has perfect plans to provide for us, and sometimes our desires fit into those plans, but sometimes they don't! When we pray, it is important to ask God for help understanding His will and plan.

Do you remember when we first met Mary, and the angel had come with the news that she would be the mother of Jesus? Remember, that was *not* in Mary's plans AT ALL! Let's peek again at how she responded. We'll use the English Standard Version of the Bible to see something important.

Use your blue pencil or marker again to double underline the words "according to your word."

 And Mary said, "Behold, I am the servant of the Lord; let it be to me according to your word." And the angel departed from her. (Luke 1:38 ESV)

Mary prayed in a way that said yes to God's plan **no matter what**. She wanted her life to be lived according to the will of God, not her own plans. I want to respond more like Mary when God asks me to do something!

IN YOUR OWN LIFE

And, just like we talked about above, God wants to hear our prayers. Not just the BIG important prayers, but He also wants us to talk with Him about our desires like Mary did at the wedding. Anything and everything—God cares about hearing it all!

Use your blue pencil or marker to circle how many of your needs God wants to supply according to Philippians 4:19.

 And this same God who takes care of me will supply all your needs from his glorious riches, which have been given to us in Christ Jesus.

(Philippians 4:19)

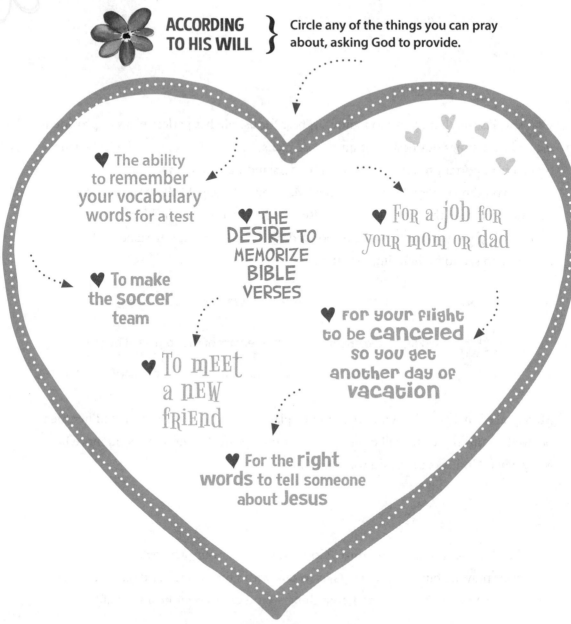

ACCORDING TO HIS WILL } Circle any of the things you can pray about, asking God to provide.

♥ The ability to remember your vocabulary words for a test

♥ THE DESIRE TO MEMORIZE BIBLE VERSES

♥ For a job for your mom or dad

♥ To make the soccer team

♥ For your flight to be canceled so you get another day of vacation

♥ To meet a new friend

♥ For the right words to tell someone about Jesus

I hope you circled all of those things. God wants you to talk to Him about everything! I mean, if God cared about the drinks at a wedding thousands of years ago, you better know that He cares about allll the little details of your life too! You can always tell Him about your desires. But be sure to ask God, "Is this in Your will?" His promise is NOT that you'll be given *anything you ask for*. God's promise is that you WILL be given *anything you ask that is in His perfect will*! He will provide for you and your family, just like He provided for Mary, Joseph, and Jesus!

Do you truly believe that?

Draw a star on the line below to represent how much you trust God to provide.

Providential Provision

1   2   3   4   5   6   7   8   9   10

"not at all"   "sometimes"   "100%—all the time!
                                                I never doubt!"

(As a reminder, this isn't to "measure" you or make you feel bad about yourself. This scale's only purpose is to help you think about your heart and make you aware of how you can grow!)

Let's be honest. It can be difficult to trust God to provide. So, let me give you a tip: **One of the greatest keys to trusting God is getting to know Him.** After all, you don't normally trust someone you know nothing about, right?!

How do you get to know God? Well, studying His Word is one of the best ways. (Hey! Since you're doing this study, you're already taking time to get to know God. Way to go, friend! Give this little hand a finger high five!)

Write one thing you've learned about God as you study the life of Mary.

⟫⟩ _____

_____

_____

You know what I'm thinking of? Jeremiah 29:11! (Do you remember that from chapter 1?!) This verse reminds you that God's plan for you is good.

Turn to chapter 1 to find Jeremiah 29:11 or look it up in your Bible. Write it below.

⟫⟶ _____

_____

_____

_____

So, as we learned in chapter 1, God has GOOD plans for you, and as we are learning now: God never plans something He will not provide for. A faithful girl trusts in God's faithfulness!

That's a lot of information, so, before we part ways, let's **zip it up**!

ZIP IT UP: What does God want me to do with it?

Is there something going on in your life that is a problem? Maybe your mom or dad needs a job, or one of your friends has been gossiping about you behind your back. Perhaps your dream of getting *en pointe* in ballet is falling through, or you've just moved to a new town and feel lonely. You want a friend. Take some time to tell God about your problem.

Write a prayer to God about your problem. Be sure to pray "according to His will."

⟫⟶ _____

_____

_____

_____

_____

_____

True Girl, let me promise you one thing. God WILL provide according to His will. In fact, sometimes, the faithful Jews who lived in Mary's day called God *Jehovah Jireh*. That name literally means, "the LORD will provide." It doesn't mean He DID provide, or He CAN provide, or He MIGHT provide. It says He WILL provide—it just might not always be in the ways you imagine or expect! He always *was*, always *is*, and always *will be* faithful!

This time with you has been so special, and I can't believe we only have one more chapter left! In our next lesson, we will see Mary in a place she probably never imagined herself. And she is sadder than she could ever have imagined being! It feels as if her soul has been pierced by a sword. Does that sound familiar? Come back for the next lesson to find out why.

CHAPTER 6

A Faithful Girl Is Loved by God through Her Suffering

Let me introduce you to someone. My friend Napoleon. I will never forget the first moment I saw him, tucked under his mama's wing. Yes, wing! Napoleon was not a human friend. He was a peacock!

Napoleon's mom was Roxy, a white peahen. She had gone missing for several weeks. Then one day, I saw her perched on a fence post. So did my 1,500-pound horse, who got to Roxy first and was pressing against her when I arrived. I wondered why she didn't fly off and protect herself. And that's when I saw a little chick, tucked in the safety of her shelter. That mama bird was immovable!

It reminded me of Psalm 91:4, which promises this of our great God: "*He will cover you with his pinions, and under his wings you will find refuge*" (ESV).

If a 10-pound peahen refused to move for a mighty horse, I promise you that God is not budging from His position of sheltering you. Whatever is troubling you today, it troubles Him too. And He intends to shield and protect you.

My dear Napoleon taught me this beautiful lesson and was my friend for 10 years. He came to my back deck each morning for a little visit and for peanuts and blueberries. If I was late with breakfast, he came to my bedroom window and called to wake me up! I nursed him by hand through a terrible parasite sickness. I bandaged up his bare back after a dog attacked him. He was always so sweet and gentle, even when what I did was uncomfortable.

I loved him.

You can probably tell that I'm writing in the past tense. Yesterday, a predator (maybe a coyote) got my sweet friend and . . . well, it was the end.

I'm so very grateful that God entrusted Napoleon to my care, but now I really miss him.

I didn't feel like writing today. I just felt like crying.

It's totally OK to have days like that. Sometimes it is even the best response to what's going on in your life.

Maybe you have lost a pet before and you know how I feel. Or maybe, even worse, a grandma or grandpa. Maybe a mom or dad. Death is very sad.

Every single time I feel the sadness of death, I remember that God did not want it to be a part of our world. And it is why we needed a Savior. Jesus is the only One who gives us hope to overcome this kind of pain in our broken world.

I want to spend our LAST CHAPTER talking about something a lot of people don't like to talk about: pain and suffering. And I want to look at how we can have hope when we experience those things.

Napoleon the peacock lived on the Gresh farm for 10 wonderful years. Every time I saw his feathers fanned open, it was a Marvelous Moment!

But, before we dive in, I want to do one last Faithfulness Lesson review! If you can recall our previous Faithfulness Lessons from memory, write them below! If you don't remember and need help, copy them from your Faithfulness Lessons page at the beginning of the book! Either way, A+'s all around!

⭐ FAITHFULNESS LESSON #1 _____

_____

⭐ FAITHFULNESS LESSON #2 _____

_____

⭐ FAITHFULNESS LESSON #3 _____

_____

⭐ FAITHFULNESS LESSON #4 _____

_____

⭐ FAITHFULNESS LESSON #5 _____

_____

Perfecto!

But wait, why have we spent this entire book learning about faithfulness? Is it even *that* important? Well, yes! Faithfulness is important because, from the beginning of time, God has been faithful to us even though humankind has been full of sin and evil. But God has never stopped loving us. He has never stopped being faithful, and we should want to be faithful to God out of gratitude for that faithfulness.

 **One of God's greatest gifts of faithfulness to us is Jesus!**

Mary was a very important part of God's plan to give us the gift of Jesus. Let's zoom out to get a better picture.

ZOOM OUT!

We talked a little bit about why Jesus came in our first lesson. Do you remember the big problem that came into the world?

Sin. Adam and Eve were the first ones to sin. But since then, there have been a whole lot of sinners.

Who has sinned? Use a black pencil or marker to circle the answer in Romans 3:23.

 For everyone has sinned; we all fall short of God's glorious standard.

(Romans 3:23)

I have sinned. You have sinned. We *all* have sinned, and because of this, we all experience separation from God and death. Sin is the reason that we feel any kind of pain or suffering.

But God did not want to be apart from us. He did not want us to suffer. So, from the beginning, He planned to fix the problem of sin. Both you and I know that Jesus was part of the super-ginormous plan to rescue the world. But what about *before* Him? What did people do about their sin way back then?

Get ready for some challenging thinking today. I want to introduce you to a really important word: *covenant*!

 { **covenant**: an unbreakable promise of commitment }

A covenant is a kind of promise, but it is also a form of unfailing love—a relationship. The love of God is so strong that even when we make bad mistakes or are sinful, He promises to still love and care for us. He is *faithful*! A covenant is kind of like His unbreakable promise to be *faithful*. Nothing can stop a covenant-keeping God from taking care of His people. He will always, without fail, help them in their time of need. No matter what!

Why?

Because He loves His people, all of the time, no matter what!

The Old Testament teaches us about the old covenant of God's promise. Now, here's the thing . . . even though God loves us no matter what, He does not like how sin hurts us. So, He gave His people the old covenant, which was made up of a longggg list of laws and rules they needed to follow to avoid sin. And if they did sin, there were laws and rules to follow to be forgiven. These included offering sacrifices when they sinned. Sometimes these sacrifices were crops, and other times they were animals. Both were things that mattered to them—true sacrifices from their lives.

A notable sacrifice was a lamb. And not just any lamb from the flock . . . it had to be a spotless lamb that wasn't wounded or scarred. An extra special one. When that lamb was sacrificed, the sins of a person or family were forgiven.

How do you think they felt seeing their spotless lambs die for their sins? How would you feel if an animal on your farm or from your home had to die so you could be forgiven?

I imagine each time that they saw a lamb die they remembered that sin causes death. (I feel that every time an animal on my farm dies!) But through that lamb's death, they were forgiven.

God never meant for the old covenant to be permanent! It was a lot of work for the Israelites to obey all the rules and laws of the covenant. God knew that humans couldn't keep up this constant sacrificial cycle. That's why He had a super-ginormous plan to rescue the world: a Savior. I can imagine every time they heard another prophecy about the coming Savior, it made them hopeful!

Let's zoom in.

ZOOM IN!

JOHN 19:16b–42

Use your brown pencil or marker to draw a cross above the word "cross" each time it appears. Circle names of any people who were "standing near the cross."

16b So they took Jesus away. 17 Carrying the cross by himself, he went to the place called Place of the Skull (in Hebrew, *Golgotha*). 18 There they nailed him to the cross. Two others were crucified with him, one on either side, with Jesus between them. 19 And Pilate posted a sign on the cross that read, "Jesus of Nazareth, the King of the Jews." 20 The place where Jesus was crucified was near the city, and the sign was written in Hebrew, Latin, and Greek, so that many people could read it. 21 Then the leading priests objected and said to Pilate, "Change it from 'The King of the Jews' to 'He said, I am King of the Jews.'" 22 Pilate replied, "No, what I have written, I have written." 23 When the soldiers had crucified Jesus, they divided his clothes among the four of them. They also took his robe, but it was seamless, woven in one piece from top to bottom. 24 So they said, "Rather than tearing it apart, let's throw dice for it." This fulfilled the Scripture that says, "They divided my garments among themselves and threw dice for my clothing." So that is what they did. 25 Standing near the cross were Jesus' mother, and his mother's sister, Mary (the wife of Clopas), and Mary Magdalene. 26 When Jesus saw his mother standing there beside the disciple he loved, he said to her, "Dear woman, here is your son." 27 And he said to this disciple, "Here is your mother." And from then on this disciple took her into his home. 28 Jesus knew that his mission was now finished, and to fulfill Scripture he said, "I am thirsty." 29 A jar of sour wine was sitting there, so they soaked a sponge in it, put it on a hyssop branch, and held it up to his lips. 30 When Jesus had tasted it, he said, "It is finished!" Then he bowed his head and gave up his spirit. 31 It was the day of preparation, and the Jewish leaders

didn't want the bodies hanging there the next day, which was the Sabbath (and a very special

Sabbath, because it was Passover week). So they asked Pilate to hasten their deaths by ordering

that their legs be broken. Then their bodies could be taken down. 32 So the soldiers came and

broke the legs of the two men crucified with Jesus. 33 But when they came to Jesus, they saw

that he was already dead, so they didn't break his legs. 34 One of the soldiers, however, pierced

his side with a spear, and immediately blood and water flowed out. 35 (This report is from an

eyewitness giving an accurate account. He speaks the truth so that you also may continue to

believe.) 36 These things happened in fulfillment of the Scriptures that say, "Not one of his

bones will be broken," 37 and "They will look on the one they pierced." 38 Afterward Joseph of

Arimathea, who had been a secret disciple of Jesus (because he feared the Jewish leaders),

asked Pilate for permission to take down Jesus' body. When Pilate gave permission, Joseph came

and took the body away. 39 With him came Nicodemus, the man who had come to Jesus at

night. He brought about seventy-five pounds of perfumed ointment made from myrrh and

aloes. 40 Following Jewish burial custom, they wrapped Jesus' body with the spices in long

sheets of linen cloth. 41 The place of crucifixion was near a garden, where there was a new

tomb, never used before. 42 And so, because it was the day of preparation for the Jewish

Passover and since the tomb was close at hand, they laid Jesus there.

Reading this passage makes my heart just want to break. Roman crucifixions were known as one of the most terrible and painful ways to die. Jesus suffered horribly on the cross.

Suffering
OF THE
CROSS

Circle all of the horrible things that Jesus experienced in today's Bible reading.

HIS HANDS AND FEET WERE NAILED TO THE CROSS. HE WAS GIVEN A REFRESHING DRINK OF WATER. HE WAS NAKED AND HIS CLOTHING WAS DIVIDED UP FOR SOLDIERS TO TAKE. HE TOLD EVERYONE HE WAS MAD. HE HAD A COMFY CROWN ON HIS HEAD. HE WAS SUPER THIRSTY, BUT THEY GAVE HIM SOUR WINE INSTEAD OF WATER. HIS SIDE WAS PIERCED WITH A SPEAR. HE DIED.

Sometimes people picture Jesus all alone on the cross, with just two criminals beside Him. But Jesus was not alone. There was a crowd of people mocking Him, soldiers insulting Him, and a few friends and followers crying. Some of them were right next to the cross.

Who does John 19:25 tell us was standing next to the cross?

Can you imagine how difficult it would be to stand next to a cross that your friend, brother, or son was nailed to? I can't. Yet, Mary stood there.

Take some time to sit and think about the emotions that must have been going through Mary's head. Put yourself in her place. How would you feel if you were her?

SOUL SUFFERING } Do you remember when we studied how Mary and Joseph took baby Jesus to the temple to dedicate Him? Simeon spoke to Mary and told her that "a sword will pierce your very soul" (Luke 2:35). Find the key words in Luke 2:35 in the word search.

SWORD   PIERCE   SOUL

```
P  N  T  G  K  R  L  K  J  S  G  M
I  O  R  W  J  U  S  O  U  L  Z  P
E  N  V  C  P  N  W  N  K  X  V  D
R  D  E  V  V  W  H  L  S  K  K  F
C  G  H  K  N  M  L  K  W  M  G  O
E  S  W  O  R  D  C  F  P  E  N  V
D  W  G  P  U  C  H  W  L  J  X  D
X  O  U  O  Y  X  V  M  P  S  Y  G
```

* For puzzle answers, look in the back of the book.

I wonder if she thought of those words when she stood by the cross, watching Jesus die. Perhaps this moment at the cross was the ultimate sword that pierced her soul. **The suffering of Jesus was also a suffering for Mary.**

But look what happens as she is standing there in deep emotional pain. Jesus—though He was in excruciating physical pain—remains faithful.

Glance back at John 19:25–27. What did Jesus do for His mother while He was suffering on the cross?

Jesus compassionately looks at His mom and remembers that she needs someone else to take care of her since He will no longer be able to do it. In His dying moments, Jesus makes plans to have His friend and follower take care of her from now on. That's our Jesus. He loves us and cares for us in our times of suffering.

This brings us to our **FAITHFULNESS LESSON #6:**
A Faithful Girl Is Loved by God through Her Suffering.

Fill in the blanks!
Faithfulness Lesson #6:

A faithful girl is _____ by _____

through her _____.

Go back to your **Faithfulness Lessons** page at the beginning of this study.
Beside #6, rewrite the sentence above.

What?! You might think: "That faithfulness lesson doesn't tell me what to *do*!" Exactly. It's easy to make being faithful to God all about us. We can fall into a trap to *do* a lot of things and follow a lot of rules. And sometimes there are things that are important to do, but mostly faithfulness is about being near Jesus so we can be changed by His love.

Mary stood near Jesus. And she was loved by Him in a time of great suffering. Yes, there was grief. Yes, there were tears. Yes, there was a cross and a grave. But, as she stood at the foot of the cross, Mary was loved. There in her pain, she experienced God's faithfulness in a special way.

There was nothing else Mary did that day at the cross. Other than just *being* there. Her job was just to be near the cross and receive the love of God.

Not long after, Jesus spoke His last words and breathed His last breath.

Go back to John 19:30 and write below Jesus' last words.

 _____

What do you think Jesus was talking about when He said, **"It is finished"**?

 _____

If you said something like, "the old covenant was over," you're spot on! I already told you that for years and years, people had been sacrificing "perfect lambs" to temporarily cover their sins and that they'd been waiting for a Savior. Well, during that time, they were hearing the prophecies about a coming Savior. And one day, John the Baptist recognized that He had finally come. I want to show you what John said when he saw Jesus.

Use a red pencil or marker to circle the word "lamb" in the verse below.

 John saw Jesus coming toward him and said, "Look! The Lamb of God who takes away the sin of the world!" (John 1:29)

Jesus was and is the *"Lamb of God who takes away the sin of the world!"*

Jesus was the final sacrificial lamb that God's people had been waiting for! When Jesus died, He said, "It is finished," to declare that the constant killing of sacrifices for sin was paid once and for all. Because of Jesus, the old covenant was no longer needed.

With a yellow pencil or marker, circle the word "covenant" in the verses below.

 But now Jesus, our High Priest, has been given a ministry that is

far superior to the old priesthood, for he is the one who mediates

for us a far better covenant with God, based on better promises.

If the first covenant had been faultless, there would have been

no need for a second covenant to replace it. (Hebrews 8:6–7)

With a red pencil or marker, write the word "new" above the word "covenant" when it first appears in the verse. Write the word "old" above the word "covenant" the second time it appears.

Through Jesus, God faithfully saved the entire world from sin and death. He has established a new, unbreakable promise of faithfulness. The new covenant was made possible through the death of Jesus. The old one was no longer necessary. No more sacrificing lambs.

Now, I want to let you in on a littttttle secret. You'll need to turn to the front cover to see it.

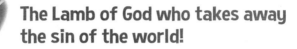

The Lamb of God who takes away the sin of the world!

Draw a picture of what Mary is holding on the cover of this book.

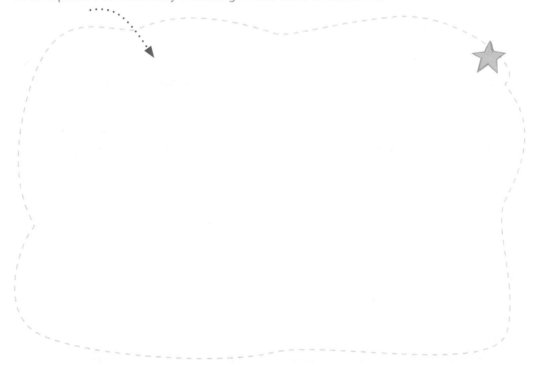

A lamb! Now, when I was working on the design for this cover, my team and I had a lot of ideas. We thought about having Mary hold baby Jesus. Buttttttt we wanted to express to you that He was so much more than a baby or even a man that grew up to be an adult. He was the perfect Sacrificial Lamb of God that could cover sin's punishment once and for all.

It was our sin that caused His suffering when He died. Our sin causes pain and suffering in our lives too. But, True Girl, God loves us in and through our suffering.

That includes our girl, Mary!

After Jesus' death, we don't know much more about Mary's life. We don't know how long she lived, when she died, or where she was buried. But we do know one thing. After Jesus came back to life, she and many of Jesus' followers were gathered together to pray with hope.

Why did they have hope? Because they had witnessed and experienced the great love of Jesus Christ. Even in their hurt and suffering.

ZERO IN: What does it mean?

We often glamorize Mary's life. But being the mother of Jesus was full of emotional pain and suffering. We easily forget how much she sacrificed to be the mother of the Savior.

You and I will also have to endure suffering because of sin.

Suffering is difficult to talk about. To our human minds, it is reallllly tricky to understand and make sense of. I've often heard people ask, "Why do bad things happen to good people?" It is a great question.

Have you ever wondered why good people have to go through hard things?

YES  NO

I know I have!

You and I live in a world with a whole lotta sin. We are reminded of this every time we hear the news. Maybe you hear about sickness or wars. Or perhaps you hear about natural disasters, like hurricanes, destroying people's homes. Sometimes, the news is just full of people being hateful to each other. The list of sad situations goes on and on. Each and every one of these is evidence of sin and evil in the world.

But . . . God loved the world so much that He sent His Son Jesus to be born by Mary. This act of love was the ultimate faithfulness.

God didn't *need* Mary, but He loooooved inviting her to be a part of HIStory, and the cool thing is, God wants to invite you into that same blessing as well! And to be loved by Him in whatever hardships you may be facing.

ZIP IT UP: What does God want me to do with it?

The Bible tells us over and over that God loves us. One of my favorite verses is Isaiah 43:4, which includes the simple words: "I love you."

Even so, I discovered that this truth is hard for some girls to believe when they have done something bad, like disobey their parents or cheat on a test. Sometimes their feelings tell them a lie about God's love.

LIE: "God only loves me when I'm good."

It's also hard to believe when we are suffering because of the sins of others or evil in the world. When bad things happen to us, we sometimes believe other kinds of lies.

LIE: "If God loved me, I would not suffer."

Have you ever believed those lies? I think most of us have at some point in our lives. Sin and evil make it difficult to *feel* God's love even though it is still there. Let me show you a verse that I use to remind myself of how much God loves me.

 But God showed his great love for us by sending Christ to die for us while we were still sinners. (Romans 5:8)

God is not surprised by sin. And when Jesus was on this earth, He told us that we'd have a lot of trouble on this planet. He knows EVERYTHING. No matter what you're going through right now, God loves you.

Will you let Him love and care for you?

IN YOUR OWN LIFE

What painful thing is causing suffering in your life right now? Is it a secret sin no one knows about? Or someone else's sin? Or just evil in the world?

How can you "stand" near Jesus the way that Mary stood at the foot of the cross?

Here are some ideas of how you can "stand" near Jesus. Circle one to try today.

♥ LISTEN TO SOME WORSHIP MUSIC

♥ Write Him a letter in a prayer journal

♥ Talk to your mom about what's troubling you and ask her to pray with you

♥ paint a picture while you listen to worship music

♥ Find a Bible verse that helps you understand your problem and write it on a note where you can see it often

♥ If you have a busy day, you can pray as you go throughout the day

♥ Tell a friend about your problem and ask them to pray

♥ walk while you pray

Whatever you circled, I hope you will do it. And that way, you can begin to experience the comfort and care of Jesus!

The day my dear Napoleon died, I was reminded again that all of the death and suffering in this world can be traced back to sin. I'm not mad about it because, as I said, it reminds me of our need for Jesus. But I was still suffering.

I knew I needed to "stand" close to Jesus. But I had a very busy day. In fact, I told Farmer Bob, "I don't even have time to cry." I decided to talk to Jesus all day long. Every now and then, I just prayed something like this: "Jesus, I'm very sad. I know You know that. Thank You for caring about the sparrows. The Bible says You do. You must care about peacocks too. Please help me feel Your nearness and to remember that You died on the cross to fix our broken world."

All day long, I felt Jesus' love—because I came near to Him. And I sensed His nearness in my sadness.

You can know that too! If you stand near Him—the Lamb of God who takes away the sin of the world!

Mary was the only person to be with Jesus the day He was born and the day He died. Jesus died 33 years after He was born in Bethlehem.

Mary was very old the day Jesus died. Some Bible scholars think she may have been about 50, which was longer than most women lived back then. It is likely that her life was almost over, but we do not know.

And Jesus? Well, I hope you know this: He didn't stay dead! Three days later, He rose from the grave and conquered death once and for all.

After Jesus came back to life and returned to heaven, the Bible briefly mentions Mary one more time. She and many of Jesus' followers were praying together in a tiny room. From this, we can see that she understood that Jesus was the Lamb of God. I believe Mary is now in heaven with Jesus, and she will never suffer again. That's what happens to anyone who believes in Jesus and gives their heart and life to Him. Mary is not in heaven because she gave birth to Jesus or because she was perfect, but because she trusted in Jesus' death on the cross as a payment for her sin. THAT is the most important lesson we can learn from Mary. Jesus was her faithful Savior.

If you have never given your life to Jesus, there's not a more perfect time than now. The next page will tell you all how to become a Christian and spend eternity with Him in heaven. And Mary. (And me!)

If you have never made a commitment to follow Jesus and make Him your Savior, that is your first step in becoming a girl of faithfulness. You cannot be faithful without Him.

If you have made Jesus the Lord of your life by asking Him to rule and reign in your heart—go in the strength of Jesus and be a *girl of faithfulness*.

Which brings me to one last puzzle! (Why not go out having fun?!)

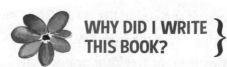

WHY DID I WRITE THIS BOOK?

With a green pencil or marker, put a checkmark ✔ next to the answer you think is correct.

Put red X's ✖ on the answers you think are incorrect.

1.
so we can **honor** and **praise mary** for her **heroic work.**

2.
To learn from Mary's faithful example and become more like Jesus.

3.
FOR NO REASON. THiS BOOK has NO PURPOSE.

* For puzzle answers, look in the back of the book.

We've been studying the life of Mary, but indirectly it's been about Jesus. **It's always about Jesus.** Never forget that, my friend!

How Do I Become a Christian?[4]

I'm glad you asked. God loves us so much He sent His Son Jesus to die on the cross for us. Though you might actually know this Bible verse by memory, I want you to read it one more time. It's an important one!

 For this is how God loved the world: He gave his one and only Son, so that everyone who believes in him will not perish but have eternal life. (John 3:16)

Why did Jesus die for us? He died because of our sin.

When we disobey God or choose to do wrong, we sin. Things like being mean, lying, or cheating are examples of sin. The Bible says that every single human who ever walked the earth has sinned. That includes you and me.

Sin separates us from God. And the Bible says the punishment for sin is death. **BUT GOD LOVES US**, so He sent His Son Jesus to die on a cross. The great news is that Jesus didn't stay dead. He came back to life with the power to forgive our sins. And, He offers us the free gift of His salvation.

I don't know about you, but I've never gotten a free gift without having to reach out to accept it. You acccpt God's free gift of salvation by *believing* in Jesus and *receiving* Him as your Savior.

To **believe** in Jesus means:

♥ to trust Jesus

♥ to know Jesus is God's Son

♥ to know Jesus saves you from your sin

♥ to be willing to give Jesus control of your life

Do you believe in Jesus?

If so, you are ready to *receive* Jesus as your Savior, which means you ask Jesus to live inside of you and be in charge of your life. Romans 10:9 reads, "If you openly declare that Jesus is Lord and believe in your heart that God raised him from the dead, you will be saved."

Have you ever received Jesus by asking Him to forgive you of your sins?

If not, would you pray this prayer now?

Dear Lord, I admit to You that I am a sinner.

I thank You for sending Jesus to die on the cross for my sins.

I ask You to forgive me of my sins. I invite You to come into my life

to be my Lord. Thank You for saving me.

In Jesus' name, amen.

Did you just pray that prayer for the first time?

If so, write the date below.

 The date I became a Christian:

_____

Congratulations!

Now, be sure to tell someone like your mom or your pastor.

They're going to be so excited!

WELCOME TO TRUE GIRL BIBLE STUDY

Mom's or Small Group Leader's Guide
for a Six- or Seven-Week Experience[5]

From before the beginning of time, God has been faithful to us. His faithfulness is interwoven through the pages of Scripture and into the lives of His people.

Mary is a prime example of His artistic tapestry. Not only is God faithful to her, but she responds to Him in faithful obedience. Her life displays a beautiful picture of faithfulness for us to learn from, making her an excellent role model for girls and women alike!

Here's how you can lead your daughter or a small group through this study: you can do it daily in a camp-style setting, or a much more digestible schedule is to tackle one chapter a week. If you're doing your first True Girl Bible study, you'll need seven weeks so you can cover the "How to Study the Bible" section during the first week. If you're a True Girl Bible study veteran, you could opt to skip the "How to Study the Bible" section and just jump right into chapter 1! In that case, you'll only need six weeks.

God will guide you in the best way to approach your discussion time, but here's what I'd suggest:

1. Get your own copy of this book and do the homework at the same pace as your daughter or small group. To be effective, you need your own copy of the book so you can study along. When I teach one of my own Bible studies online, I also do the homework in real time so that my heart is in tune with what God wants me to learn. In doing so, I'm emotionally and spiritually prepared to guide others through the content. It is challenging to be led by the Spirit and lead others if you're not engaged with God's Word in the same intimate way they have been. So, dive right on in together!

2. Select two key conversation questions from each chapter. One question can be from a core passage of Scripture in the *Zoom In & Out* section. This will help you discern what they've grappled with mentally in their studies. The second question can be from the *Zero In* section. This will help them verbalize and share where they need practical and emotional help. Just have fun gabbing about God's Word (and maybe include your favorite snack or dessert)!

3. Pray with your daughter or small group. Based on what they share each week, spend some time praying together. I also encourage you to pray for them throughout the week—in doing so, you'll have the privilege of seeing greater fruit. Pray for their heart to be open, softened, and receptive.

Encouraging Bible study for older users. For girls ages 10–12, this book is a challenge, but very age-appropriate. For far too long, we have been expecting far too little of children when they study their Bibles. While I hope this is a fun experience with puzzles and interactivity, my goal is for them to get a taste of how wonderful it is to work diligently toward understanding and applying God's Word. Over and over, I'm asked how to make something easier for a tween or a teen. But let me encourage you: Why not try letting them jump into the deep end and experience the thrill?! If they need a life preserver, send them one, but you might be surprised how well they can swim in the deep end of Scripture.

Simplifying the study for younger users. For girls ages 7–9, look for the flower icon.

Each time they reach this, it's time to stop! These icons divide chapters 1–6 into two parts, making one day's worth of homework time shorter and easier to digest. This means that younger girls can schedule two homework sessions each week instead of one so that they finish the chapter at the same time as older girls would. Ultimately, *you* know what's best and can curate the best study plan for your girl(s).

Finally, press into FAITHFULNESS! Rely on the Lord and Him alone to help you grow in this area. May the young girls who follow you learn faithfulness—not just from the pages of this study, but from your life!

Dannah Gresh
Founder, True Girl

ANSWERS TO PUZZLES

Answer to *"Prophecy Puzzle"* on page 25:

E	W	R	M	Y	M	M	T	T	G	N	O	K	R	T	Q	Z	L
N	J	M	S	N	H	D	W	J	Q	E	O	F	L	F	W	W	C
D	F	N	O	E	A	R	T	H	L	Y	F	A	T	H	E	R	V
O	Z	G	K	I	N	G	D	A	V	I	D	R	W	K	O	U	I
G	W	X	I	A	J	C	Z	C	L	B	Y	E	N	G	S	X	A
H	N	O	Y	J	E	U	W	Z	Z	B	B	Y	G	Z	K	J	T
I	S	G	M	C	B	E	T	H	L	E	H	E	M	Y	H	D	Q
Q	O	R	U	A	F	B	Q	U	R	F	W	Q	Q	N	P	N	S
Y	W	U	F	Y	N	X	M	M	I	R	A	C	L	E	S	T	I
Z	K	C	G	Q	S	X	V	U	J	D	P	A	A	M	A	Z	Y
Y	S	Z	R	Q	U	A	E	F	U	L	T	Q	C	B	H	F	R
C	T	M	R	I	H	P	K	Z	X	L	B	U	B	K	T	C	B

Answer to *"Mary's Dilemma"* on page 28:

Answer to *"Mary Magnifies"* on page 48:

Answer to *"Why Did Mary Go To See Elizabeth?"* on page 46:

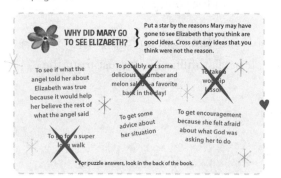

Answer to *"Practicing Immediate Obedience"* on page 74:

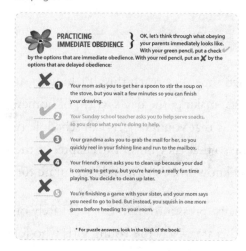

Answer to *"Truth Teller"* on page 75:

DISOBEDIENCE

Answer to *"The Puzzle Pieces of Prophecy"* on page 82:

Answer to *"Water Into Wine"* on page 104:

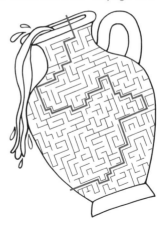

Answer to *"People and Places"* on page 84:

Answer to *"Suffering of the Cross"* on page 120:

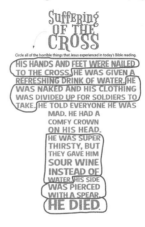

Answer to *"Mary's Mission"* on page 90:

Answer to *"Soul Suffering"* on page 122:

Answer to *"Perfect Provision"* on page 101:

Answer to *"Why Did I Write This Book?"* on page 130:

1. so we can **honor** and **praise mary** for her **heroic work**.

2. To learn from **Mary's** faithful example and become **more** like Jesus.

3. FOR NO REASON. THIS BOOK HAS NO PURPOSE.

NOTES

1. This introduction is adapted from Dannah Gresh, *Ruth: Becoming a Girl of Loyalty* (Chicago: Moody Publishers, 2001).

2. Dannah Gresh, *Lies Girls Believe: And the Truth That Sets Them Free* (Chicago: Moody Publishers, 2019), 32.

3. Nancy DeMoss Wolgemuth, "Mary Was a Humble Woman," *Revive Our Hearts* podcast, December 24, 2014, https://www.reviveourhearts.com/podcast/revive-our-hearts/mary-was-humble-woman/.

4. " How to Be a Christian" section taken from Dannah Gresh, *Lies Girls Believe: And the Truth That Sets Them Free* (Chicago: Moody Publishers, 2019), 57–59.

5. Parts of this leader's guide are adapted from Dannah Gresh, *Ruth: Becoming a Girl of Loyalty* (Chicago: Moody Publishers, 2001).

JOIN US FOR OUR ONLINE BIBLE STUDIES

EXPERIENCE FREEDOM THROUGH GOD'S TRUTH

Dig deep into God's Word with an online Bible study from True Girl!
Each study has a unique focus that will help you and the young women in your life fight the world's lies as you grow closer to Jesus. Join us for an upcoming livestream study, or access our library of recorded studies that you can view on demand.

STUDIES YOU'LL LOVE

TEACHERS YOU CAN TRUST

DANNAH GRESH   STACI RUDOLPH   SHANI MCKENZIE   JANET MYLIN

REGISTER AT: mytruegirl.com/onlinebiblestudies

For more resources and events
for tweens, go to mytruegirl.com.

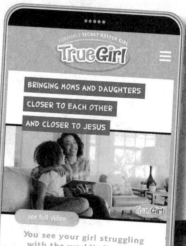

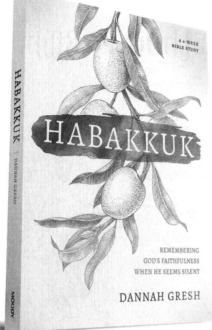

A 6-WEEK
BIBLE STUDY

HABAKKUK

REMEMBERING
GOD'S FAITHFULNESS
WHEN HE SEEMS SILENT

DANNAH GRESH

Your Guide to
Experiencing Joy
as You Live by Faith
Rather than Fear in
Difficult Times.

THE BOOK OF HABAKKUK is about learning to believe that God is good
and maintains control even when there is so much evil and tragedy in the
world around us. Though this book is often overlooked during times of
peace and prosperity, it has tended to be studied when believers needed
to learn how to talk to God during epic events.

dannahgresh.com/habakkuk

ISBN: 978-0802419804

MOODY
Publishers®

From the Word *to Life*®

Learn the 4-Z Method of Bible Study

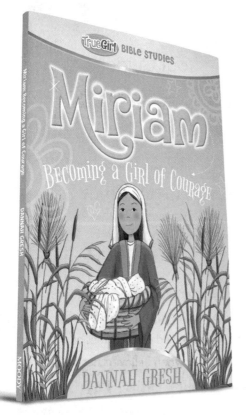

ISBN: 978-0-8024-2241-5

ISBN 978-0-8024-2222-4

Zoom. Zoom. Zero. Zip!

mytrugirl.com